PENGUIN BOOKS

SPEAKING OF FAITH

Krista Tippett is a journalist, former diplomat, and creator of the weekly public radio program *Speaking of Faith*. She has hosted and produced the show at American Public Media since its inception as an occasional series in 2000. It is now heard globally via podcast and Internet and carried by over two hundred public radio stations nationwide.

www.speakingoffaith.org

Praise for *Speaking of Faith*

"In a day where religion—or rather, *arguments* over religion—divide us into ever more entrenched and frustrated camps, Krista Tippett is exactly the measured, balanced commentator we need. Her intelligence is like a salve for all thinking people who have felt wounded or marginalized by The God Wars."
— Elizabeth Gilbert, author of *Eat, Pray, Love*

"We need to take religion seriously. We need to give voice in our national life to religious and non-religious people alike who understand, as Tippett does, that the crooked line dividing good from evil runs through each of us . . . We should be grateful to Tippett not only for amplifying voices of sane faith but also for modeling in herself a public theology that manages to derive faith out of doubt and hope out of paradox."
— Stephen Prothero, author of *Religious Literacy*

"At a time when professional contrarians like Sam Harris and Christopher Hitchens take the meaning and mystery out of religion, Krista Tippett is a welcome voice of literate faith."
— *The Dallas Morning News*

"*Speaking of Faith* is a chronicle of ideas. . . . It is also a memoir with a narrative thread that makes this book as compelling as any novel. In her book as on the radio, Tippett is an intelligent observer, sophisticated and compassionate. Reading Tippett is like attending a dinner party with some of the most interesting minds in America and standing at the elbow of the hostess as she introduces each friend." —*Catholic Online*

"Krista Tippett is a master of nuance for whom the great questions of belief transcend the simple answers that modern religion too often supplies. This is a vision of faith as a grand and unifying struggle with the very nature of being, and it is both deeply thought and deeply felt. It is a reminder, in a time when too much that is evil happens in the name of creed, that the search for God can be transcendent and exquisite. Tippett's prose is lyrical and elegant, and her formulations are wise and profound; her arguments should move the secularist and the dogmatist alike to a new vision of peace."

—Andrew Solomon, National Book Award–winning author of *The Noonday Demon*

"There is no more trustworthy guide to the challenges of faith in a dangerous world than Krista Tippett. With this book she has created an original and authentic place in the great debate of our time."

—Yossi Klein Halevi, journalist and author of *At the Entrance to the Garden of Eden: A Jew's Search for God with Christians and Muslims in the Holy Land*

"As Tippett takes on issues from the science-and-religion debates to the future of progressive Islam, she shows herself to possess the same 'imaginative intellectual approach' that she admires in some of her interview subjects." —*Publishers Weekly*

"Overflowing with gems of wisdom, the book offers thoughts on matters related to faith, religion and spirituality worth pondering as deeply as one's imagination allows."

—Diane Raabe, Gather.com

"A thoughtful, wide-ranging and highly approachable introduction to the possible in spirituality. It's one thinking person's open door to faith in the twenty-first century."

—*St. Louis Post-Dispatch*

"The brilliance of Krista Tippett's idea is to trust people to use the first person singular, to commit themselves with passion and clarity as they enlarge our urgent national conversation."

—Martin E. Marty, Professor Emeritus of American Religious History, University of Chicago

"*Speaking of Faith* is of monumental importance and a source of light in a day and age when the darkness of intolerance, ignorance and hate blinds humanity from itself."

—Dr. Khaled Abou El Fadl, professor of law, UCLA, and author of *The Great Theft: Wrestling Islam from the Extremists*

"Krista Tippett manages to claim the middle space—a very large, inclusive space—where most of us live most of the time, a place in which we must ponder and live the abiding questions of faith, doubt and meaning that have been at the heart of human experience from time immemorial."

—Patricia Hampl

"*Speaking of Faith* is a beautiful book written by one of public radio's most beloved and respected interviewers. In *Speaking of Faith* Tippett embodies the humility and perseverance of the seeker and shows us beyond doubt how questions and not answers can be trusted to lead us closer to ultimate mystery. A wonderful read in a polarized world."

—Dr. Rachel Naomi Remen, clinical professor, UCSF School of Medicine and author of *Kitchen Table Wisdom* and *My Grandfather's Blessings*

SPEAKING
of FAITH

Why Religion Matters—
and How to Talk About It

KRISTA TIPPETT

PENGUIN BOOKS

PENGUIN BOOKS

Published by the Penguin Group
Penguin Group (USA) Inc., 375 Hudson Street, New York, New York 10014, U.S.A.
Penguin Group (Canada), 90 Eglinton Avenue East, Suite 700, Toronto,
Ontario, Canada M4P 2Y3 (a division of Pearson Penguin Canada Inc.)
Penguin Books Ltd, 80 Strand, London WC2R 0RL, England
Penguin Ireland, 25 St Stephen's Green, Dublin 2, Ireland (a division of Penguin Books Ltd)
Penguin Group (Australia), 250 Camberwell Road, Camberwell, Victoria 3124, Australia
(a division of Pearson Australia Group Pty Ltd)
Penguin Books India Pvt Ltd, 11 Community Centre, Panchsheel Park,
New Delhi – 110 017, India
Penguin Group (NZ), 67 Apollo Drive, Rosedale, North Shore 0632,
New Zealand (a division of Pearson New Zealand Ltd)
Penguin Books (South Africa) (Pty) Ltd, 24 Sturdee Avenue,
Rosebank, Johannesburg 2196, South Africa

Penguin Books Ltd, Registered Offices: 80 Strand, London WC2R 0RL, England

First published in the United States of America by Viking Penguin,
a member of Penguin Group (USA) Inc. 2007
Published in Penguin Books 2008

10 9 8 7 6 5 4 3 2 1

Grateful acknowledgment is made for permission to reprint the following copyrighted works:
    "God speaks to each of us as he makes us" from *Rilke's Book of Hours: Love Poems to God*, trans-
lated by Anita Barrows and Joanna Macy. Copyright © Anita Barrows and Joanna Macy, 1996. Used
by permission of Riverhead Books, a member of Penguin Group (USA) Inc.
    Prayer ("Grant us, our Father, your grace") from *Justice and Mercy* by Reinhold Niebuhr, edited
by Ursula M. Niebuhr (Harper and Row, 1974). Reprinted by permission of the Estate of Reinhold
Niebuhr.
    Prayer ("I no longer ask you for either happiness or paradise") from *One Generation After* by Elie
Wiesel. Copyright © 1965, 1967, 1970 by Elie Wiesel. Reprinted by permission of Georges Bor-
chardt, Inc. on behalf of the author.

THE LIBRARY OF CONGRESS HAS CATALOGED THE HARDCOVER EDITION AS FOLLOWS:
Tippett, Krista.
    Speaking of faith / by Krista Tippett.
      p. cm.
    ISBN 978-0-670-03835-0 (hc.)
    ISBN 978-0-14-311318-8 (pbk.)
    1. Spiritual life.   2. Religion.   3. Religion and politics.   4. Religion and culture.   I. Title.
    BL624.T56   2007
    200—dc22   2006036074

Printed in the United States of America
Set in Adobe Garamond   Designed by Spring Hoteling

For Aly and Sebastian
With gratitude for your patience
And all my love

Contents

ACKNOWLEDGMENTS   xi

CHAPTER ONE
Genesis: How We Got Here   1

CHAPTER TWO
Remembering Forward   18

CHAPTER THREE
Rethinking Religious Truth   41

CHAPTER FOUR
Speaking of Faith   109

CHAPTER FIVE
Exposing Virtue   172

CHAPTER SIX
Confessing Mystery   206

INDEX   233

ACKNOWLEDGMENTS

YEARS AGO I STARTED KEEPING A list called "People Who Believed"—friends and colleagues who encouraged my conviction that it was time for intelligent, in-depth conversation about religion in American public life. I've been borne up these last few years by the faith and practical care of many others, and I'm grateful to them all.

Collegeville is where my current vocation and passions began to take shape, and I have a sense of homecoming whenever I return to the communities of Saint John's Abbey and Saint Benedict's Monastery. Father Roger Kasprick was especially helpful in the final months of this project. I will forever be grateful to Father Kilian McDonnell for allowing me to conduct an oral history of the ecumenical institute he founded. His marvelous poetry, the new vocation of this chapter of his life, inspired this chapter of mine. Patrick Henry and Dolores Schuh made me welcome in the life of the ecumenical institute and became cherished colleagues.

Molly McMillan made the writing of the first incarnation of this book possible a decade ago.

Saint Benedict's and Saint John's also provided space for me to think and write across the years, as did the delightful ARC retreat center in Cambridge, Minnesota, and the magical Anam Cara Writer's Retreat in Ireland. I was also given beautiful places to rest and write by my dear friend Nell Hillsley—one of the first who believed—as well as the late great Betty Musser, Bill and Susan Sands, and Ron and Carol Vantine. Penny and Bill George provided much appreciated hospitality and wisdom in the late stages of this project, as they have for many years. John Stone, Bill Manning, Larry O'Shaughnessy, Pat Cook, and Julie and Charlie Zelle have also been "angels" to *Speaking of Faith,* and friends.

Many people read this manuscript and made it better at some stage, among them Michael Tippett, Patrick Henry, Patricia Hampl, Laurisa Sellers, Nell Hillsley, Molly McMillan, Ellen Davis, Barry Cytron, Martin Marty, Billie Alban, Omid Safi, Richard Mouw, Robert Pollack, Bill Buzenberg, and Kate Moos. Bill was the first person in public radio to believe in *Speaking of Faith,* and knowing him has enriched my life immeasurably in the intervening years. Brian Newhouse and Marge Ostroushko helped shape and launch *Speaking of Faith* in its infancy. Kate Moos is my professional rock, and one of the people I most admire in the world. I am so proud of what we've accomplished together, and of the deep friendship, collegiality, and creativity of our team: wonderful, talented people and producers Colleen Scheck and Jody Abramson; online genius Trent Gilliss; and senior producer Mitch Hanley, a genius at the art and craft of radio. This book reflects our common work. I've also been grateful for the tremendous support of American Public Media, especially from Bill Kling, Sarah Lutman, and Mary Sutherland.

Finally, thanks to my agent Tom Grady and to Ellen Garrison, who provided great editorial guidance in the book's final stages. Without my editor Carolyn Carlson's vision, wisdom, persistence, and persuasion, I would have written a far inferior book. Thank you for believing I could do this, even when I did not.

God speaks to each of us as he makes us,
Then walks with us silently out of the night.

These are the words we dimly hear:

You, sent out beyond your recall,
Go to the limits of your longing.
Embody me.

Flare up like flame
And make big shadows I can move in.

Let everything happen to you: beauty and terror.
Just keep going. No feeling is final.
Don't let yourself lose me.

Nearby is the country they call life.
You will know it by its seriousness.

Give me your hand.

—RAINER MARIA RILKE, *Rilke's Book of Hours:*
Love Poems to God, TRANSLATED BY ANITA BAR-
ROWS AND JOANNA MACY.

SPEAKING OF FAITH

Chapter One

Genesis: *How We Got Here*

———

Why are we now all——believer as well as atheist, in public and in private—talking about religion? Why is spirituality suddenly everywhere? Why has faith become so passionate—and so dangerous? Some say, I know, that religion is the cause of our worst divisions, and a threat to democracy and civilization here and abroad. The truth is more broadly and deeply rooted in the human psyche and spirit. The great traditions have survived across millennia because they express insights that human beings have repeatedly found to be true. But they are *containers* for those insights—fashioned and carried forward by human beings, and therefore prone to every passion and frailty of the human condition. Religions become entangled with human identity, and there is nothing more intimate and volatile than that, especially in an age of global transition like ours. Our sacred traditions should help us live more thoughtfully, generously, and hopefully with the tensions of our age. But to grasp that, we must look anew at the very nature of faith, and at what it might really mean to take religion seriously in human life and in the world.

What most of us surely want, whether we are religious or not, is for the religious voice in our public life to be more constructive—to reflect the capacity religion has to nourish lives and communities. I reject the kind of sweeping prognostication that has become popular in recent years and fueled fear and paranoia: doomsday scenarios of impending theocracy, phrases like a "clash of civilizations." I spend my days probing beneath the surfaces of stridency and the headlines of violence. I'm drawn to the contours and depths of what I call "the vast middle"—left, right, and center, between the poles of competing certainties that have hijacked our cultural discourse. In the vast middle, faith is as much about questions as it is about answers. It is possible to be a believer and a listener at the same time, to be both fervent and searching, to honor the truth of one's own convictions and the mystery of the convictions of others. The context of most religious virtue is relationship—practical love in families and communities, and care for the suffering and the stranger beyond the bounds of one's own identity. Christianity puts an exacting fine point on this, calling also for love of enemies. These qualities of religion should enlarge, not narrow, our public conversation about all of the important issues before us. They should reframe it.

In the pages that follow, I describe adventures of life and conversation that have opened my imagination—spiritual, political, intellectual, and personal. I illustrate a way to speak about faith that defuses the usual minefields. I explore the light my conversation partners shed on the great issues of our time, from the depths of their knowledge and experience in the world. They are theologians and scientists, educators and physicians, social activists and poets. We trace a powerful and creative and humbling line between theology and human experience—between religious ideas and real life. This is religion as it works in the lives of the many, not in the debates and headlines of a few.

I was born on the night John F. Kennedy was elected president. So I arrived more or less with the '60s, but too late to experience the underlying hope and whimsy of the times. I came of age to the unraveling of dreams. All of my earliest public memories, the defining public events of my childhood, are of violence and tragedy, and always attached to admirable faces: John and Robert Kennedy; Martin Luther King, Jr.; young men coming home bloody and broken from Vietnam. I grew up with a strong but deeply conflicted sense of politics as the primary arena of human action—of social power and of human frailty, of light and dark secularized yet of biblical proportions.

But life on this side of a new millennium and my interviews of recent years have altogether changed the way I would tell the story of the momentous decade of my birth. Much of its hope as well as its tragedy yielded to irony and dead ends. The mighty Soviet Union was in the end a Trojan horse. The flower children raised stockbrokers. The Vietnam War succumbed to popular protest, but it has been succeeded by other wars in which it is more difficult to discern a clear moral stance. And between and among these political events, religious seeds were being planted that are coming to fruition and shaping the global present. Kennedy's Catholicism and Martin Luther King, Jr.'s theology were as pivotal for our culture as their politics. The Immigration and Nationality Act of 1965 quietly flung our demographic doors open to all of the world's religions. The vast, unresolved change set in motion in the mid-1960s by the Second Vatican Council is an animating factor in the global north-south divide that has followed the east-west Cold War. And the Barry Goldwater presidential campaign of 1964 marked the little-noticed entry of evangelical Christians into conservative national electoral politics.

Nevertheless, in those same years western intellectuals were foretelling and urging the end of religion. This line of thinking has a long modern tradition—from the Enlightenment thinkers and Karl Marx to Sam Harris, Richard Dawkins, and Christopher Hitchens in the early twenty-first century. Their critiques are near-fundamentalist in tone, in the spirit of our age. The secular sages of the 1960s were less combative. They believed that as human beings grew more modern and technologically advanced and our societies more plural, religion would simply retreat to the private sphere. Perhaps it would disappear altogether. Harvard's Harvey Cox published his runaway bestseller *The Secular City*, praising the joys of post-religious culture, in 1965. On April 8, 1966, *Time* magazine asked on its cover, "Is God Dead?" This was not erudition, as we now know, but myopia—a lapse of perspective.

Religion never ceased to matter for most people in most cultures around the world. Only northern Europe and North America became less overtly religious in the course of the twentieth century. In characteristic fashion, we saw ourselves as the rule, not the exception. For decades religion was simply not treated seriously by those who were running governments and writing history and driving industry and defining the issues. Religion, as the Boston University sociologist Peter Berger muses, became something "that was done in private between consenting adults." That is to say, we began to bracket our ways of making meaning and defining personal conscience out of our spheres of action in the world.

Religiously, spiritually, I was a child of my time. I grew up in Oklahoma, the granddaughter of a Southern Baptist preacher. Through him I experienced the drama of faith, but my parents had turned their backs on his stern rules for a fallen creation. We went to church on Sunday. Monday through Friday I was raised to win, to perfect myself, and to do so in the American way of accomplishment and accumulation. My father listened to election returns as my mother gave birth. He was a political operator in a culture where politics is ruthlessly provincial, a blood sport. I watched him wage wars on the pages of newspapers and by way of radio ads. As an Oklahoma Democrat, he was more conservative than most Massachusetts Republicans. But he imprinted me with what, in the wider world, are hybrid instincts. In that decade of my birth, he was a true believer in civil rights and the war on poverty. I loved his passion and idealism. They became entangled with cynicism and pain in the years of my childhood in which good men and high ideals fell one by one, shot down all too easily and finally by other men.

Later I landed in the heart of divided Europe, confronting the Cold War clash of good and evil as a young journalist and then at the level of diplomatic and strategic high policy. This was the era of the Berlin Wall and the Iron Curtain and terrifying enemies who, in contrast with our current enemies, now appear wondrously civil and contained. Granted, they had thousands upon thousands of weapons of mass destruction—long range, medium range, short range, trained on our major cities—but we knew this. We had our weapons trained on them too, in commensurate numbers. And when I arrived in divided Berlin in the early 1980s, no one imagined the whimper with which the Soviet empire would end. In neighboring Poland, future president Lech Walesa's Solidarity movement had just been crushed. In Czechoslovakia, future president Vaclav Havel was a safely imprisoned dissident for life. And the wall running through Berlin—a material symbol of the ideological "Iron Curtain" that cut through the heart of the ancient continent—appeared as the shape of forever, an unshakable truth of our lifetimes. I hold on to these memories now as a reminder that there is at any given moment much reality we do not see, and more change possible than we can begin to imagine. I believed then that all of the important and interesting problems in the world were political, and all of the solutions, too. And for a while I threw myself body, mind, and spirit at this conviction.

But I changed my mind. This book is a chronicle of a change of mind, and of a discipline of listening that keeps my mind and my spirit stretching. There are places in human experience that politics can not analyze or address, and they are among our raw, essential, heartbreaking, and life-giving realities.

I returned to America from Europe in the early 1990s as my generation and others were rediscovering a hunger for spiritual depth, for religious moorings. I studied theology to learn whether I could reconcile religious faith with my intelligence and the breadth of my experience in the world, whether faith could illuminate life in all its complexity and passion and frailty. I decided that it can. I have found a vast and vivid landscape of others who share this discovery. The spiritual energy of our time, as I've come to understand it, is not a rejection of the rational disciplines by which we've ordered our common life for many decades—law, politics, economics, science. It is, rather, a realization that these disciplines have a limited scope. They can't ask ultimate questions of morality and meaning. We can construct factual accounts and systems from DNA, gross national product, legal code, but they don't begin to tell us how to order our astonishments, what matters in a life, what matters in a death, how to love, how we can be of service to each other. These are the kinds of questions religion arose to address and religious traditions are keepers of conversation across generations about them.

And in this handful of years since I began to think and speak about faith in a new way, the world has realigned itself once again. Religion has moved from the sidelines to the center of world affairs and American life. After the last few decades of U.S. politics, and after September 11, 2001, Western pundits and policymakers and citizens have awakened collectively to the fact that religion never went away. Indeed, it remains a force that animates lives and nations and history—for better or for worse. Religious identities and spiritually fueled passions are shaping this post–Cold War century as ideologies defined the last. And nothing could be more unrealistic—or more dangerous—than the prescription that reasonable people should abandon religion for its sins. For every shrill and violent voice that throws itself in front of microphones and cameras in the name of God, there are countless lives of gentleness and good works who will not. We need to see and hear them, as well, to understand the whole story of religion in our world. This book is one kind of beginning—and an exploration of my sense that religious people and traditions themselves contain the most powerful critique and correctives we have against religion's excesses.

This book is also in part a response to questions my listeners have asked of me. How did I come to be asking the questions I ask, how has my own spiritual sensibility evolved, and how do I see the world differently through my life of listening across the world's traditions? I have struggled to write and remain faithful to my philosophy of journalism and my theology of speaking of faith. I bring one voice at a time onto the air. Everyone speaks out of his or her own life, knowledge, and truth—and never for all Christians, Muslims, or Buddhists, for God, Qur'an, or the Bible. I'm indebted to them all, and they have all formed my vocabulary and imagination and approach. They have filled the often vague, sometimes divisive words "faith" and "religion" and "spirituality" with luminous connotations and nuance. They have also helped me understand that the words "atheist" and "agnostic" are narrowing boxes in our culture as well. Spiritual questions don't go away, nor does a sense of wonder and mystery cease, in the absence of a belief in God. Nonreligious people are some of the most fervent seekers of our age, energetically crafting lives of meaning. But in these pages I will concentrate on religion per se, especially the three monotheistic traditions—Judaism, Christianity, and Islam—at the source of so much vitality and confusion in the world right now. I also cast an eye toward Buddhism, which has cultivated ancient spiritual technologies with a special appeal for modern people of many faiths and no faith at all.

Like any journalist, I also have my own bearings in life, my own experience in the field I cover. The economics correspondent has a bank account; the political analyst votes; and I am a person of faith. My own starting point and perspective are grounded in Christianity. As I reflect openly on my own theology in these pages, I'm very aware that Christianity and its divisions are at the heart of many modern-day civic struggles. Traditional Christian instincts also profoundly, if often subconsciously, shape Western culture's emerging encounter with the wider world and its many religions.

Chapter two, "Remembering Forward," takes its title from a line I love in Lewis Carroll's *Through the Looking Glass:* "It's a poor sort of memory that only works backwards." This captures some of the profound and concrete learning in my life of faith and conversation. As Einstein laid out in scientific terms, time and the experiences it holds and the wisdom it imparts work more like circles than lines. The Bible treats time as multidimensional: past, present, and future in fluid, enlivening interplay. This is also an insight of modern psychology, like so much of sacred wisdom. The visionaries and leaders of all of the great religious traditions, sometimes stubbornly and sometimes wisely, are always looking back in order to move forward.

In "Remembering Forward," I trace the formative spiritual trajectory of my early life in and out of faith between frontier Protestantism and secular global politics. My Southern Baptist grandfather embodied stern, rigid religious principles that ceased to make sense as I moved into a world of greater complexity. Yet the memory of him tethers my understanding of the human religious impulse in our time. It humanizes my analysis of the broadly evangelical Christianity that has become an axis of our national life in recent years. And I could not have gravitated in early adulthood to a better place than Germany to indulge the late twentieth-century view of religion as extraneous and dying. Seeds of religious thought that I encountered in those years and have later explored by way of radio—the ideas of Dietrich Bonhoeffer and Elie Wiesel and Reinhold Niebuhr—help me think about the radically changed geopolitical and religious landscape we inhabit now. After Germany I became religious again, but with an attention to the irony and paradox that mark human experience and religious ideas at their most supple and creative.

In chapter three, "Rethinking Religious Truth," I explore the intellectual and spiritual substance of religion that is often misrepresented by religion's critics and even religious people themselves. We have to think about knowledge itself differently—the insides and edges of words and ideas, the richness of their forms—to understand the nature of religion and the work of theology in which we might all engage. There is a richness when intelligence and faith intertwine. I first discovered this while living in England, and later through formal theological study at Yale. I read the Hebrew Bible seriously, for example, to grasp the artificiality of the evolution/creation debate. And I find the insights of modern physics as helpful as those of religion as I consider the challenges that evil and suffering in the world pose to the very notion of faith. Ideas from the worlds of art and science repeatedly give me new, creative ways to think about the "rationality" of religious modes of thought. The writings of Thomas Merton and T. S. Eliot and Julian of Norwich have a place in this chapter, as do conversations with scientists in many fields, and a reexamination of the spiritual legacies of Charles Darwin and Albert Einstein.

In chapter four, "Speaking of Faith," I explore the narrative way of speaking about religion and ethics that I translated into journalism for radio and that has a power to reframe some of our most difficult public conversations. My listeners tell me that they adapt and carry on this conversation in their communities and workplaces and families; that it enables them to speak across predictable divides. I describe the long sacred view of time of Benedictine monastics who first taught me to listen and speak about God in a new way. I trace my learning curve as I've approached large questions that have entered our culture in the years since I created *Speaking of Faith:* What is the spiritual core and theology of Islam? Where is the moderate, nonviolent Muslim voice? What is the proper role of religion in American public life, and is it threatening the value of separation of church and state? How can we take religious passions seriously in regions of the world where religion seems to be the heart of the problem? Voices in this chapter include the theologian Roberta Bondi, the Quaker educator Parker Palmer, the religious scholar Karen Armstrong, the Abbas and Ammas of the ancient desert; and religious perspectives on global realities from Muslim lawyer Khaled Abou el Fadl, Israeli journalist Yossi Klein Halevi, and Indian journalist Pankaj Mishra.

In chapter five, "Exposing Virtue," I explore how attention to life-giving spiritual ideas and practices might address and reframe our deepest modern confusions: What happens when religion goes wrong? Why don't lived hope and virtue appear as relevant as destruction and suffering? How can we retrain our eyes and ears to see the compelling, reconciliatory heart of religion in the midst of better-publicized despair? Thinkers and activists like the journalist Bruce Feiler, environmentalist Wangari Maathai, theologian Miroslav Volf, physician David Hilfiker, and cosmologist George Ellis contend in practical ways with subjects we all long to address but encounter too often by way of stories and statistics that frighten and overwhelm: poverty; global inequity; ecological degradation; and, not least, the problem of religious violence. This chapter also includes reflection on the lessons of South Africa's process of Truth and Reconciliation, our polarized conversation about gay marriage, and "the core moral value of beauty."

And in chapter six, "Confessing Mystery," I propose a renewed appreciation for mystery as an antidote both to relativism and to extremism. At their orthodox cores, religious traditions themselves ask us to hold our notions of earthly certainties and transcendant mystery—what we believe we know, and what we can never know for sure in time and space—in an exacting, creative tension. This creative tension could help reform our common life. It could be a key to rooting strong identities and life-giving truths while living generously in a world of plurality.

In this final chapter, I also delve in a more personal way into the religious questions and struggles that continue to form me, the theological lessons that parenting brings, and the imprint my life of listening leaves on me. I've known the failure of love and the failure of hope in my own life in these years since I discovered theology. I have been helped by my ever-deepening understanding that faith as a whole encompasses and blesses human vulnerability. The kind of journalism I do is, as much for myself as for others, about looking beyond the horrors of the evening news to the redemptive stories that are not being told, to ways of being in the world that keep sense and virtue and the possibility of healing alive in the middle of the world's complexity. In this chapter I draw on the wisdom of the physician Rachel Naomi Remen, the author Annie Dillard, Pentecostal sociologist Margaret Poloma, the Benedictines of Collegeville, and the Zen master and poet Thich Nhat Hanh.

I offer this chronicle of my questions and those of others, and of glimpses of answers and truth, with reverence and humility. I offer it in defiance of the competing certainties of our public life. And I offer it as a contrast to the religious stance more intent on holding correct positions than on how one treats both friends and enemies along the way. I offer it in celebration of concepts indigenous to human reality and the resilient human spirit if not to politics and often not religion. In the pages that follow, I trace the qualities of true religion, of the human spirit, of God perhaps, as I've come to listen for them in the company of others.

Chapter Two

Remembering Forward

———

In the mid-twentieth century, before the temporary death of God, before Jerry Falwell and Pat Robertson, there was such a thing as "public theology" in American life, and Reinhold Niebuhr was its most trenchant voice. In my life of conversation, he is one of the thinkers most often cited as an influence by a vast array of modern people. He is one of the religious voices who guides my thought about what has gone wrong with religion in our common life and how it might go right again. Niebuhr, who died in 1971 at age seventy-eight, did not propose religious ideas as policy.

Rather, he articulated a theological point of view to challenge thinking on every side of every important question. He understood theology as a discipline by which religious people could temper and deepen political life, not inflame it. In his day, Niebuhr influenced presidents and Supreme Court judges, social activists and poets. He was unclassifiable politically—or rather, he was alternately called a liberal, a hawk, a reactionary, a pacifist. In his "Letter from Birmingham City Jail," Martin Luther King Jr. quoted Niebuhr as an influence as he developed his idea of Christian nonviolent resistance. Niebuhr's books had grand, evocative titles: *The Nature and Destiny of Man, Moral Man and Immoral Society, The Irony of American History.* He was also a prolific author of essays and sermons. He drafted a prayer during World War II that was later adapted as the Serenity Prayer of Alcoholics Anonymous. And he was famous for other prayers that captured his theology succinctly:

> Grant us, our Father, your grace, that, seeing ourselves in the light of your holiness, we may be cleansed of the pride and vainglory which obscure your truth; and knowing that from you no secrets are hid, we may perceive and confront those deceits and disguises by which we deceive ourselves and

our fellowmen. So may we worship you in
spirit and in truth and in your light, see
light.

As pragmatically as any other figure in modern memory,
Niebuhr connected grand religious ideas with messy human
realities. He coined the term "Christian realist"—a middle
way between religious arrogance and religious impractical-
ity. People in our society long for a middle way between arrogance and irrelevance. And whether they are religious or
not, they long for religion to live up to its best ideals. These
would include a humility about the fact that while there may
be a transcendent God and a transcendent good, these only
intersect imperfectly with the complexities of politics and
social order and human failings. Like Niebuhr, I take my analysis of religion in the world—its excesses and redemptive possibilities—from its source in the richness, mystery, and mess
of human life. He opened his classic work of theology, *The
Nature and Destiny of Man,* with this succinct, perfect line:
"Man has always been his own most vexing problem." *Tragedy, irony,* and *paradox* were among Niebuhr's treasured
words, and I first learned their meanings between the American frontier and the Germany that formed Niebuhr's
forebears.

The Oklahoma in which I grew up was an outpost of

the Southern Baptist empire. But the faith of my childhood was evangelical before that label carried the identity politics or conservative associations of today. In fact, until the early twentieth century, *Protestant* and *evangelical* were interchangeable terms. And biblically conservative Christians were as likely to be engaged in causes of social justice as of personal morality. In the 1920s in Oklahoma, Gospel preaching helped galvanize a short-lived but dramatic "farmer-labor" revolt against big business. During the same era, the northern Baptist Walter Rauschenbusch famously preached the "Social Gospel"—a fusion of piety, evangelism, and concern for the poor. The primary sin of American culture, as Rauschenbusch saw it, was not private moral transgression but collective selfishness. He developed his Christian socialist theology during a decade in New York's "Hell's Kitchen." Though Rauschenbusch is largely forgotten in popular culture today, his analysis of the tensions between capitalism, justice, and social morality influenced Mahatma Gandhi, Martin Luther King Jr., and Desmond Tutu.

But as the century progressed, a more theologically liberal Christianity picked up the mantle of social justice and defended it with critical biblical scholarship, altogether questioning the transcendent power of God. This specter, compounded by economic depression and war in the world, led conservative Protestants to begin to concentrate less on saving society and more on saving souls. Their time, like ours, was also marked by breathtaking technological advance that magnified both progress and danger. The new evangelicals concentrated on the personal moral sphere over which an individual could have control.

My maternal grandfather, the Reverend C. T. Perkins, emerged from that tradition. I called him Gaggy. My later fascination with religion had surely to do with his singular integrity among all the members of my family. Here I use that word *integrity* strictly; he had it all together, for better or worse. He discerned certain truths about the nature of the universe, and he lived by them. They both clarified and constrained his range of vision and movement. My mother grew up forbidden to dance, swim, go to movies, wear pants, or play cards.

But she did not subject me to his rules and so I was free to be intrigued by him. I could never buy in to the popular idea in our family that he was a tyrant. He was funny. He told jokes. He laughed easily. He bought a farm after he retired from evangelizing, planted a vegetable garden, and lovingly built wooden birdhouses. Even as he preached hellfire and brimstone, he had a sense of play. He was a man of God with a sense of humor—and to this day that is a combination I admire and seek out. Also, though he only had a third-grade education, my grandfather possessed a strange prodigious intelligence. He could perform complex mathematical feats in his head. After his death I inherited the bibles he studied and preached by—mighty leather-bound King James versions with feather-thin pages—and found page after page marked with notes, annotations, cross-references, every margin full of observations that speak to a love for the life of the mind. From an early age I sensed this in myself, an unlearned pleasure I could take in ideas, the written word, and the thoughts in my head, their powers of making sense.

I believe that Gaggy held intellectual clarity and personal pleasure in a truce with his faith. He kept them a respectable distance away from beliefs and rules he had accepted as true and beyond question, indeed dangerous to think through to the end. He was as passionate physically as he was spiritually, and handsome to the end of his life, with sharp cheekbones and an elegant bald head. He had eloped with my grandmother Mary, a petite dark-haired beauty at the piano in one of the churches where he evangelized. "Exactly nine months" later, so I heard many times, she gave birth to a stillborn boy on their kitchen table. C. T. and Mary believed they would never have children until my mother came along, like a miracle, nine years later. There was a fear in Gaggy as large as his laughter, as vigorous as his mind. And the Christian faith, as I learned it from him, saw human beings as weak creatures set loose in a world awash with dangers. The wages of sin—as the Apostle Paul said it, and my grandfather heard this connected exclusively with individual, often sexual, morality—was death. He carried this conviction as a burden, a grave personal responsibility to stave off eternal damnation one life at a time.

My children love this story about my grandfather, rich with echoes of Eden and apocalypse: once, in the summertime, while I was helping him do chores around the yard of a little mission church in his charge, I found myself in a shed with a large, dark coiled snake. I raced out of the shed, screaming. Gaggy came to my rescue of course. He harassed the snake into the open with a hoe and it reared up as tall as him in memory, or taller, looking him in the eyes. I can still conjure that moment in my mind's eye to this day: the preacher and the serpent, salvation and damnation embodied and facing off. After a few heart-stopping failed swings, Gaggy severed the snake's head. This is my emblematic memory of my grandfather.

I spent much of my childhood in church. It was the center of social life, not just religion, in our small town. I spent hours with the Bible and felt God speaking to me straight off the pages. Faith helped me live with the tension between the smallness of the world around me and my intense inner sense of a larger beyond. It helped keep that tension alive. In this way it grounded me in reality, not just mystery. But my grandfather's rules and beliefs did not add up as I grew older. I came to find the disjunction between the thoroughness of my mind and the limitations of church teachings intolerable. I would only be able to return to faith after I concluded that the stories and vocabulary and symbols of the faith of my childhood could withstand and contain my questions and ideas. Christianity itself would yield and expand, making room for even larger questions beyond my wildest imagining. I needed faith to be as generous, as open to creativity and intellect and humor, as my grandfather at his best.

But I hold to my memories of his complexity—his fear and fallenness along with the humanity and virtues of that faith of my childhood—against stereotyped images of evangelical Christianity that are at large in our culture now. The rock-solid, certain aspects of my grandfather's faith bequeathed me a spiritual inheritance. They are the foundation upon which my questions and ideas now are planted. I learned to trust in an overriding sense behind the universe. I learned to look for grace and for truths that revealed themselves at times baldly but just as often between the cracks in my ability to see and hear what is important. Above all, I understood belovedness to be woven into the very fabric of life. "For God so loved the world," began the pivotal verse of my grandfather's faith, John 3:16. "Jesus loves me" was a simple sung refrain of my childhood, an antidote to the darkness of night and the larger terrors of the world. This message is spreading rapidly across the world today—in Asia, Africa, and Latin America more vigorously than in North America—and most often with an evangelical or Pentecostal flavor. Erudite analyses, for all their merits, rarely take note of the power of a sense of belovedness as an antidote to fear.

When I left Oklahoma to go to Brown University in 1979, my grandfather consoled himself with the fact that Brown had been founded in Roger Williams's Rhode Island—a Baptist counterpart to Congregationalist Yale and Harvard, Episcopal Penn and Columbia, and Presbyterian Princeton. But Roger Williams, as I would later learn, was a freewheeling freethinker, as much a restless agitator as a man of principle. He was Baptist in part because he had rejected everyone else's faith. To his credit, he welcomed people of all religious persuasions to Rhode Island and so did Brown, after his example, from the first. And until 1937, Brown had a Baptist clergyman as its president. But by the time I arrived in Providence, the twentieth century had made its secular mark. The religion of my childhood felt bound to a particular shape of the known world. In this place, this world of heady thought and personal experimentation, it felt irrelevant.

In my first semester, I did study Kierkegaard, the nineteenth-century Danish philosopher who explored the passions of human life as a critique of both Western rationalism and religious abstractions. And in my last semester at Brown, I studied Dietrich Bonhoeffer, the German theologian and ethicist executed by the Nazis for his part in a plot to assassinate Adolf Hitler. I adored both of these thinkers, experiencing them as intellectual and spiritual friends, as I've always thought of books and authors I've loved. But their gorgeous theology and immense grappling with God, the world, and the church bore little resemblance to the practice of religion as I knew it. And in the global dramas of the first three decades of my life, religion played a minor role, a supporting role at best. Sin and salvation seemed abstractions against the battles playing themselves out on a secular map of the world. The compelling, life-defining divisions of the age were not between heaven and hell. Nuclear weapons threatened the end of life as we knew it. Academically and then personally I was drawn to Europe, and to Germany in particular, as a center of the cosmic struggle of that time—one culture sliced into two competing worlds.

For six years of my life, I became immersed in what earnest scholars called "The German Question." At the age of twenty, I took part in an experimental project at Brown—a semester in Communist East Germany, in the port town of

Rostock on the Baltic. This was my introduction to Germany. There I saw the human underside of the arms race and the human cost of tyrannical ideology. After college I spent a year on a Fulbright scholarship in Bonn, West Germany's sleepy happenstance of a capital city, in 1983. I arrived there along with a controversial new generation of nuclear weapons, the Pershing II and cruise missiles, which unleashed a massive anti-American peace movement. One of Kierkegaard's favorite words was on everyone's tongue in Germany that year: *Angst*. In German this translates as "fear," but on the streets of Bonn and Hamburg that autumn, it was more like Kierkegaard's core existential anxiety—a state of mind, a paralyzing collective panic. After the missiles arrived and settled into their bunkers and failed to ignite World War III, *Angst* dissipated, and I moved to Berlin as the *New York Times* stringer and a freelance foreign correspondent. I became fluent—more so in German than in English—in Cold War politics and military strategy. I was intoxicated by the importance of the issues that filled my days and nights. But ambition was not what drew me to Berlin and kept me there. I had circled back to West Berlin to be close again to the East.

People who visited East Germany in those years always used the same words to describe it: *bleak* and *gray*. But as time passed I saw nuance within those relentless browns and grays. I saw lives that wrested color from them. After three months in East Germany, I traveled to West Berlin with my wondrous Western passport, and the neon lights hurt my eyes. I spent hours walking along the Berlin Wall, which I had visited before as a tourist and considered as a geopolitical monument. I cried this time; I loved people whose lives it enclosed. I could walk up and touch it from this side. In places on this western side it was painted bright, whimsical even, with graffiti. It was only twelve feet high. But on the other side it was made monstrous, unscalable, by tank traps and men with guns. The same men observed me through binoculars from watchtowers now. I hated them; I pitied them. Most of them were about my age, on compulsory military service. Their lives also ended at this ring of asbestos and concrete.

Thumbing through the diary that I kept in those months I stumble on this sentence: "I had decided I believe in God because the world makes too much sense. I still believe in him (one feels the void of faith here), but no longer that the world makes sense."

The despots of the twentieth century—Chairman Mao, Pol Pot, Stalin, Hitler—had no need of God to unleash their unparalleled magnitude of bloodshed and terror. Yet they did employ devices of religious zeal. East Germany, like all the Soviet empire, was defiantly atheist. But for all practical purposes the state was a deity; Marx and Lenin were sacred texts; the Soviet Union was holy land. The feeling of faith could not be imposed, only its trappings; but public doubt was not brooked. Contradictions of doctrine were punishable by imprisonment, exile, or death. East Germany adapted the economics of Marxism-Leninism as successfully as any country; this was, after all, the birthplace of Karl Marx. But that society's spiritual deficits were more evident precisely because of its economic success. No one starved in East Germany, but as a culture, as a state, it utterly lacked vitality. Marxism-Leninism was reverent with material need but reckless with the human longing for meaning, the hunger for beauty. So very unlike me—for whom the whole world was opening up—my East German friends lived without an anticipation of surprise or adventure in life. They lived without a deep experience of hope. And hope, like love, is one of life's redeeming experiences. Hope, or its absence, shows on you.

The American response to the Communist threat also had strong overtly religious, near-missionary elements. We forget this too, though its echoes reverberate through our mission in the world now, against very different foes. Certainly, as Reinhold Niebuhr recognized and cautioned in the last century, Americans have historically, from the beginning, interpreted the wealth and progress made possible by geographical isolation and natural bounty as signs of divine blessing. This intensified as, while fighting Communism's atheist evil, we further internalized capitalism and democracy as divinely ordained good. I can see my own long fixation on Germany as an extension of the religious world view of my childhood. Germany's division was about the world's brokenness, and my passion—now secularized and recast in political terms—was for salvation. And like me, for better or worse, Germany was in love with ideas. German history is full of flights of brilliance, great thinkers determined to find the overarching system to gather up the whole of reality and order it. Kant, Hegel, Marx, and Nietzsche aspired to nothing less than this. There is a touching aspiration to supreme good, a theological insight gone awry, in these bold attempts to perfect the original creative act: to impart order to a world of chaos. In the twentieth century, a terrible distortion of that same impulse made Germany the perfecter of holocaust.

I first met the original memoirist of the Holocaust, Elie Wiesel, in that vanished divided Berlin. He survived the Nazi reign of terror, but his sister and father and six million other Jews succumbed. I had become a journalist by this time, schooled by some great *New York Times* reporters. Wiesel was visiting Berlin for the first time since the Holocaust as a guest of the German government. He had asked to meet with a group of young Germans. He was nervous about this meeting, and afterward he was visibly shaken. Together with another journalist, I sat with Wiesel and his wife. "I had never before considered," he said, "that it could be as painful to be a child of those who ran the camps as a child of those who died in them."

I was astonished that Wiesel, a victim of German genocide, was open to seeing the tragedy and resilience of the human spirit on every side of it. His words unsettled and moved me. They stirred conclusions I was struggling to articulate in that country with a tortured past and present. I was thoroughly caught up in the enduring strategic, geopolitical consequences of Germany's descent into Nazi terror. Yet through Elie Wiesel's eyes, goals like human redemption and healing—and not just retribution, economic rebuilding, and balances of power—also appeared urgent. I felt that Wiesel's words belonged on the front page of newspapers, that they should be shouted to the world. But I believed this had nothing to do with God. Wiesel's faith, as he wrote in *Night*, had been consumed forever by the flames of the ovens at Auschwitz. Two decades would pass before I could speak with him again, and be surprised again by his words.

The voice of the Christian theologian Dietrich Bonhoeffer also broke into my thinking in those years. There is no clearer voice of Christian theology formed by the tragedies and terrible mysteries of history than Bonhoeffer. And because of the way Bonhoeffer grappled toward theology by way of politics, I was able to find him intriguing and respectable. A pastor and a pacifist, the son of a gracious German family, he became involved in the July 20, 1944, plot to kill Hitler. He was executed in the German system of terror that Elie Wiesel survived.

Before Bonhoeffer died, though, he brought weighty, creative, challenging theology into the world. In my radio life now, Bonhoeffer's name like Niebuhr's punctuates my conversations with wildly different people, recurs as a refrain in countless interviews and in the most unlikely places. I've found that many others take solace and courage in a phrase of Bonhoeffer's that emboldened me even in the years in which I was defiantly not a religious person. He wrote from prison in 1944, "I'm still discovering right up to this moment, that it is only by living completely in this world that one learns to have faith. . . . I mean living unreservedly in life's duties, problems, successes and failures, experiences and perplexities. In so doing we throw ourselves completely into the arms of God."

As Fascism overtook his country and German Christianity itself, Bonhoeffer helped to found the Confessing Church, the center of Protestant resistance to Fascism. For a time, he led an alternative seminary. And while he wrote an opus about Christian ethics, he threw himself behind a plot to assassinate Adolf Hitler. The times in which he lived drove him to reconsider the essential meaning of faith and the nature of God and ethics. "The will of God," he concluded in a sentence that would make my grandfather shudder, "is not a system of rules established from the outset. And for this reason a man must forever re-examine what the will of God may be. The will of God may lie deeply concealed beneath a great number of possibilities."

At the center of Bonhoeffer's writing from prison was an assertion that the church—religion itself—fails us, fails at its own highest aspirations. But he didn't want to let God go, and he didn't want to abandon Christianity, for the lamentable failings of human beings and institutions created in their image. He insisted, even as he faced death, that Christianity brings essential questions and insights into the world—insights that the world needs, and that it will constantly reinvent and rename even as institutions betray them. We've pushed God to the boundaries, he wrote, where the rest of our knowledge gives out. We've consigned God to the gaps in our scientific understanding, to the wings of our action. We've reserved prayer for when our best efforts fail. Bonhoeffer said we would have to rethink the very forms and vocabulary of faith if we were to keep it alive in the center of life—in the middle of the village, as he liked to analogize, not confined to ever-shrinking boundaries or held within the walls of the church. Such ideas came back to me as I stretched my own thinking about faith in my years after Germany. I stored them up, as we often do with spiritual words and writings that matter. They don't penetrate until we are ready to hear them.

Dietrich Bonhoeffer was hanged at Flossenbürg concentration camp in Bavaria on April 9, 1945, just weeks before the collapse of the Reich. His death seemed to me a puzzle, a piece of religious irony. Wasn't this a failure of God, a rebuttal of the very idea of God? Yet some irrational aura of triumph—defying my sense of time as flat and contained—surrounded Bonhoeffer's legacy. I could not fathom this when I lived in Germany, and I did not try.

A practical irony took hold, in my years in Berlin, that I felt most alive on the bleaker, grayer, eastern side of the wall. My most beloved friends were a Russian painter, Kolya, and his exuberant translator wife, Christel. They introduced me to other friends—teachers, doctors, writers—carving out spaces of camaraderie and comfort beneath the exterior of that semitotalitarian world. I spent many evenings with them in darkly lit pubs thick with cigarette smoke and poetry and yearning and dreams made more beautiful by the fact that the dreamers solidly believed they would never, ever come true. Many of their desires were heartbreakingly easy in the world I would return to before midnight: to ride a motorcycle across America; to publish an essay; to see Rembrandt in the Louvre. In those hours drawn out by drink and food and music, few inconsequential words were spoken. Joy and laughter were deepened because they were tinged with sadness at other experiences lost to possibility. Vicariously, in that now-vanished Communist capital, I was learning the exhilarating intensity that can accompany human catastrophe. I struggle not to glorify it now in memory. But it was teaching me about the human condition. It was pressing me to question definitions of power and meaning that would eventually haunt me and drive me from Berlin. Success and satisfaction could rarely be sought by way of public accomplishment in that world. The state superimposed its will on nearly every detail of its citizens' outer lives. But in response, ordinary people defended and grew their inner lives defiantly. They poured creativity and energy into their intimate circles of family and friends. They discerned truth, or betrayed it, at deeply personal cost.

Back home on the western side of the wall, I walked through an idiosyncratic Berlin side door to diplomacy. At twenty-five, I became a special assistant first to the senior American diplomat in West Berlin and then to the U.S. ambassador to Bonn, a Reagan appointee. A cross section of the social and political glitz of the eighties—self-made billion-aires, royal hangers-on, Hollywood society—passed through my life in my last year in Berlin. I sat around dinner tables with famous people, beautiful people, powerful people, and also around conference tables with men, mostly men, who were moving nuclear missiles around like Tonka Toys on a map of Europe.

I felt increasingly torn between my empathy with human life in the East and a strategic view from the West that was turning me into a hawk. I could have certain conversations in those years more fluently in German than in English—conversations about Pershing IIs and cruise missiles, Soviet deceptions and intransigence, the SALT II Treaty. But where did the resilience of the human spirit express itself at this level of policy, I wondered, and could this level of policy address the spiritual underpinnings of human experience? Are the "life" and "death" threatened by nuclear missiles worth living or dying for? Where is my energy most needed, and where will it be most effective? These kinds of questions dogged me through my years in Berlin. I knew that just as worlds of human dignity flourished beneath the East's surface of want, there were layers of human want beneath the surface of Western plenty that I was engaged in defending. Communism crushed many souls, but it ennobled others. Capitalism did the same, but with preferable, subtler devices. I saw this dramatically in Berlin's juxtaposed worlds, but I recognized it also when I traveled home.

I was also rattled by the contradictions I observed in the lives around me. There was a chasm between the genuine importance of the issues at hand and the moral maturity of some of the people who were defining those issues and literally running the world. In our time, *immorality* is a shrunken word, suggestive only of sexual impropriety. But up close to power at a young age, I experienced a problem deeper and more basic: powerful people often had impoverished inner lives. Foreign policy giants who could deliver brilliant speeches on strategy and disarmament were in private shockingly immature, emotionally stuck in adolescence. In this they contrasted ironically with my friends behind the Berlin Wall. These Western leaders had unlimited possibilities for self-creation and public accomplishment. This came with a temptation and a trap, it seemed, to invest inordinate energy in the projection and compromise of public life and to wither inside. And I began to sense that this would prevent them from ever getting to the root of the human problems they were addressing by way of high policy.

I was drawn to Germany originally because the world's great symbolic divisions swirled at its heart. But it sent me away with an attention to the human life that swirls stubbornly, full of contradictions and beauty and grief and defiance, beneath the grandest categories of history and politics.

I have ever after been wary of systems, with "isms" employed to classify whole cultures that after all consist of people. The nuclear arms race is now a chapter in history books, but terrorism thrives in its place. In our time, we analyze global realities and culture wars with new categories, defining and dismissing whole swaths of human life in terms of "fundamentalism" and "liberalism" and "terrorism." These labels only tell us partial truths. We must use them humbly, guardedly, Niebuhr would say, aware of the limitations of our own vision and of our own capacity for misunderstanding and self-deception.

Remembering forward, I also see that the East-West division of the world masked other simmering global gaps of cultural stability and human equity. The collapse of that wall in Berlin that I knew so intimately led in some very direct way to the fall of other invisible walls that had kept the West shielded from the brew of religion, ethnicity, and politics in much of the rest of the world. The United States and the Soviet Union projected their struggles onto what we classified as "the Third World." We avoided reckoning with the final unraveling of colonialism in that same period, and we complicated its aftereffects. But entrenched patterns of human misery, global poverty, corruption, and despair have now risen to the surface. They drive conflicts and crises that touch us all.

In Berlin I learned that transcendent goals like peace and justice are always made possible, or rendered impossible, by the patterns of the human heart. The human condition is the reality around which political life revolves—and upon which it falters. Even the highest levels of diplomacy and geopolitical strategy are about treating the symptoms of humanity on the loose. This fact is made more complex, not more transparent, in our era where religious passions and identities overtly fuel political conflict—where, in other words, the human heart is openly, wantonly involved. And now I'm engaged in probing for human and spiritual dynamics beneath the present surfaces of rancor. I'm able to do so because I learned, in the years after I left Berlin and in my subsequent life of conversation, how to take religion seriously—how to see its substance and its weight in the world and its meanings in human life, both light and dark.

CHAPTER THREE

RETHINKING RELIGIOUS TRUTH

———

I'VE COME TO UNDERSTAND RELIGIOUS TEXTS and traditions as keepers of truth more openhearted and realistic than many of the arguments against them and the practices in their orbit. We have to think about truth and about knowledge itself differently—the insides and edges of words and ideas, the richness of their forms—to understand the nature of religion and the work of theology, the human attempt to pin God, however fleetingly, down to earth. In many ways, religion comes from the same place in us that art comes from. The language of the human heart is poetry.

Music is a language of the spirit. The métier of religious ideas is parable, verse, and story. All of our names for God are metaphor—necessary license, approximation, and analogy. Our sacred texts burn with that knowledge and dare us to use all of our faculties of intelligence and experience and creativity. But we forget this; our fact- and argument-obsessed culture is deaf to it, blind to it.

The British author Karen Armstrong has written sweeping, scholarly works—*A History of God; The Battle for God*—that have helped many understand the history and force of religion in the post-9/11 world. I treasure the conversation I had with her because she was able to think with me in intellectual terms about the fact that theology, words about God, very respectably begin elsewhere and circle back to the language of reason. Early in her own discovery of the world of religious thought, she tells me, she had a great gift. She was reading a wonderful and erudite book and lit upon a footnote that explained in dry academic language what a religious historian was supposed to do. He—"I think they assumed it would be a he rather than a she"—was supposed to practice "the scientia of compassion"—that is, knowledge acquired by compassion.

And in this little footnote the author said
that you must not lead the discussion of a

religious idea or a theology or a personality such as Muhammad without being able to find out what lay at the root of this—not to dismiss these ideas out of hand from a superior viewpoint of post-enlightenment, Western rationalism, but to divest yourself of that rationalistic outlook and enter the minds of these mystics and sages and poets and keep on asking, "But why? But why?" And filling up with scholarly knowledge the background until you come to the point where you can imagine yourself feeling the same, or believing the same as them, until basically the intellectual idea learns to reverberate with you personally.

We miss the essence of great religious figures, Karen Armstrong insists, if we imagine them sitting, uttering a list of doctrines. "And our theology," she says, "should be like poetry." I ask her what she means by that.

A poet spends a great deal of time listening to his unconscious, and slowly calling up a poem word by word, phrase by phrase, until something beautiful is brought forth into the world that changes people's perceptions. And we respond to a poem emotionally. And I think we should take as great a care when we write our theology as we would if we were writing such a poem, instead of just trotting out an orthodox formula, or an orthodox definition of God, or a catechism answer—so that when people listen to a theological idea, they feel as touched as when they read a great poem by, say, Milton or Dante. And we should take as great care with our religious rituals as if we were putting on a great performance at a theater—because theater indeed was originally a religious ritual designed to lead us to transcendence, instead of mechanically going through motions of our various rites and ceremonies—trying to make them into something absolutely beautiful and inspiring. I do see religion as a kind of art form.

This is a lovely and important way to understand why we can't compare faith flatly to reason and declare it intellectually inferior. Its territory is the drama of human life, where art is more precise than science, where ideas are lived and breathed. Our minds can be engaged in this realm as seriously as in the construction of argument or logic, but in a different way. Life and art both test the limits and landscape of argument and logic. We apprehend religious mystery and truth in words and as often, perhaps, beyond them: in the presence of beauty, in acts of kindness, in silence. Silence is an endangered quantity in our time—though monasteries and retreat centers are filling up with a new kind of pilgrim, modern people stealing away for solitude, starved for silence. Silence, embraced, stuns with its presence, its pregnant reality—a reality that does not negate reason and argument, but puts them in their place.

Quiet and submission born of fatigue were the beginnings of wisdom for me after Berlin. Fresh air and the sun's warmth, almond and apricot and lemon trees, fresh bread and strong Spanish coffee, the ocean in late afternoon—these were its elements. I handed my resignation to the ambassador and his wife, believing I was headed for Washington in a matter of months. But first I decided to go back to one of the most beautiful places I had ever visited—Deia, a village ringed by mountains on the Spanish island of Mallorca. I put my furniture into storage and packed two suitcases, out of which I would live, as it turned out, for the next two years.

Alone in Deia, I began to realize how tired and confused I was. I felt this physically, before I could turn it into ideas and words. This was salutary for me. I had made my way through the world up to now—and this is still my greatest virtue and vice rolled together, my demon and my gift—by my wits alone, headfirst. I forced myself out of bed at daybreak every day and rushed a silly, shallow novel about Berlin into being. I thought this was my purpose for being there and the accomplishment I would have to show for it. But in moments I thought were not productive, I looked out the tiny window by my desk. I saw mountain, sky, and air that dwarfed nuclear weapons and the life and death they seemed to threaten. I breathed deeply. The world began to realign itself more generously, or rather my vision did. None of this was logical, none of it made sense.

Early, quite early, I put away most of the books I had brought along. I read Rilke, whom I had loved for years and whose gorgeous, iconoclastic language felt right in this place. I memorized one line of his poetry that soothed and energized me at once. It might be a motto of my work now: *ich glaube an alles noch nie gesagte*—"I believe in everything that has not yet been said." I reread his advice in *Letters to a Young Poet*,

> to have patience with everything unresolved
> in your heart and to try to love the questions
> themselves as if they were locked rooms or

books written in a very foreign language. Don't search for the answers, which could not be given to you now, because you would not be able to live them. And the point is to live everything. Live the questions now. Perhaps then, someday far in the future, you will gradually, without even noticing it, live your way into the answer.

From there I went to England to visit a Scotsman, Michael Tippett, whom I had first met and fallen in love with a year earlier. I stayed, and in May 1989 I married him. I moved with my new husband to a serene English village called Codford St. Mary. I read and wrote in the back bedroom of a rented eight-hundred-year-old cottage, looking out at roses that bloomed from March to November. The English mystics plucked their spirit from this damp, fertile countryside I now inhabited, miraculous shades of green as far as the eye could see. All of these strange, magnetic characters spoke to me: the anonymous author of the powerful, barely comprehensible *Cloud of Unknowing;* the wise hermit Julian of Norwich; the lowly, medieval Brother Lawrence, who found that prayer could consist of washing dishes. They described contours of mystery within reality, the multidimensional reality that had been outside my realm of perception in frantic, self-important, political Berlin. Their discoveries did not match mine precisely, but they emboldened me.

I was not religious yet, not for many months. I was an explorer. But irresistibly I was drawn to theology—the articulation of words about God. My mother tongue was Christianity. But I resolved that I would only return there with open eyes, rigor of thought and speech, and the same powers of reasoning that I expected of myself in the rest of my life. Karen Armstrong quotes T. S. Eliot throughout her autobiography, *The Spiral Staircase*. His finely wrought spiritual despair showed her a way to let faith go and ultimately approach it again with a new integrity. Eliot—a convert to Christianity from reason alone—also helped me with his poetic grasp of religious essentials and the sense of irony he maintained even at his most devout:

> *Of all that was done in the past, you eat the fruit,*
> *either rotten or ripe*
> *And the Church must be forever building, and always*
> *decaying, and always being restored.*

> *. . . Has the Church failed mankind,*
> *and has mankind failed the Church?*

If indeed mankind had failed the church and not the other way around, I could separate my disillusionment with the church from my new discoveries. I could construct a theology unhindered by cultural norms and old subjective grudges. I didn't have to equate faith itself with my grandfather's anguishing blind spots, or tragic nonsensical violence between different Christians in nearby Ireland, or the perfunctory, unwelcoming piety of the vicar of the village I now inhabited. I could decide for myself what it was about, and live accordingly.

In a small, captivating essay about Genesis, *Creation and Fall,* Dietrich Bonhoeffer described biblical stories as "ancient, magical pictures that we need alongside modern technical, conceptual pictures if we are to become wise." In England, I began to see in these ancient, magical pictures a response to the deepest real-world confusions of my years in Berlin. I was aching with spiritual and moral questions I could scarcely articulate. I was reading mystical texts and Buddhist texts and they thrilled me. But this Bible on the bookshelf, long unopened, was the foundational text of my spiritual homeland and mother tongue.

The Bible, as I read it now, is not a catalogue of absolutes, as its champions sometimes imply. Nor is it a document of fantasy, as its critics charge. It is an ancient record of an ongoing encounter with God in the darkness as well as the light of human experience. Like all sacred texts, it employs multiple forms of language to convey truth: poetry, narrative, legend, parable, echoing imagery, wordplay, prophecy, metaphor, didactics, wisdom saying. In the Christianity of the modern West, we've largely left the vivid storytelling of the Hebrew Bible, the Old Testament, in Sunday school. We've consigned it to the world of childhood figuratively and literally. And in our time a superficial Christian rendering of these biblical texts underpins false dichotomies that plague our public life—chasms we've set up between sacred text and truth, between idealized views of the way human beings should behave and the complex reality of the way they do.

But when I came back to read the biblical text after many years away, I began to love the Hebrew Bible fiercely for the fact that it tells life like it is. It has no fairy-tale heroes, only flawed, flamboyant human beings as prone to confusion as to righteousness. Like us millennia later, they had trouble reconciling the political and the private, the sexual and the societal. King David—the forefather by whom the New Testament theologians traced Jesus' lineage—was, as the text tells it, brilliant and charismatic and passionate. He held God's favor. David was at once a great leader and also an adulterer. He was a military hero, and yet he sent the husband of his mistress to the front lines to die. These facts about him stand together and in tension with an air of sadness in the biblical narrative. They are neither reconciled nor do they cancel each other out.

Or consider Lot, who is famous in Sunday schools around the world for heeding God's command to leave the sinful Sodomites without looking back, while his weaker-willed wife gave in to nostalgia and was turned to a pillar of salt. We've internalized the unforgivable sins of Sodom and Gomorrah as sexual, and contemporary religious voices routinely equate private sexual sin with the moral decline of our nation. But in the Bible itself, that equation is inferred rather than stated. It states that not a single righteous person could be found among the Sodomites, and this was the reason for their destruction. There is one scene in which Sodomite men attempt to lure other men from Lot's household out into the street with them, presumably for sexual purposes. Our hero, Lot, offers his daughters instead. But in a later biblical reference and analysis of the nature of the Sodomites' sin—one of very few—the prophet Ezekiel says that they were condemned because they had "pride, surfeit of food, prosperous ease, but did not aid the poor and needy." What if, with reference to Ezekiel, we began to understand the depravity of "sodomy" to be about a nation's neglect of its poor?

One of my favorite characters in the Bible is also one of the most human and flawed. Jacob, the son of Isaac, the grandson of Abraham, is a quintessential late bloomer, conniver, and egoist. The Bible calls him "clay footed" and yet, through foibles and false starts, God's beloved. He tricks his brother out of his inheritance. He later falls in with another trickster, his future father-in-law, who cons him into marrying the sister of the woman he loves. He works slavishly, marries both sisters finally, and becomes a successful man. In midlife, full of both pride and regret, Jacob heads home to face his demons and past mistakes. He makes his way across the land in which he has spent his adulthood back to the land of his childhood. His sins were great and his absence has been long, and he is terrified of what will greet him on the other side.

Jacob crosses the Jabbuk river. And in a moment cathartic for the sweep of monotheistic spiritual history to follow, he there encounters a mysterious man whom he afterward recognizes as a messenger of God or God himself. The "man" wrestles with Jacob, even putting his hip socket out of joint. Jacob wrestles back. "I will not let you go," he tells this stranger, who turns out to be the very source of his life, "until you bless me." At daybreak, he receives his blessing and a new name. Jacob becomes *Israel*—a word that suggests one who strives, or wrestles, with God.

This is a story beloved by many who have struggled with the gap between real life and religious ideas. True biblical faith expands and deepens as it incorporates mistakes, questions, catastrophes, and changes of mind and heart. Like Moses who "quarreled" with God, Jacob embodies the intense interplay of devotion and struggle at the heart of Jewish tradition. I've come to find in Jacob's story a model for grappling honestly and productively with sacred text itself. It is true of the entire Bible—and perhaps of any sacred text for its believers—that if you sit with these bare-bones stories, pick over them, retell them, they begin to grow—take on nuance and possibility—before your eyes. One layer of meaning is lifted and another reveals itself. You sense that the text would respond to every conceivable question. In other words, if I stick with these texts—if I wrestle with them and insist on a blessing—a blessing will come. The only limitation is my time, my powers of imaginative concentration, and my capacity to listen to the interpretations of others.

It is a crazy irony of Christianity's divisions that those traditions that hold the text most sacred sometimes discourage the God-given powers of the human mind to read and interpret. And those that encourage the life of the mind have sometimes left the text behind. The copious ink in my grandfather's Bible suggests to me that he read it carefully enough to stumble upon its intriguing contradictions. He must have seen that the God he feared was by turns a wrathful tyrant and a hopeless romantic, less omnipotent in the sweep of things than vulnerable at his core the way all fathers sometimes are. Gaggy had not been taught to question the text in that way, but I like to think that he held such questions in his tempted and passionate and playful heart as a kind of puzzle. In Codford St. Mary where I moved hesitantly toward the church again, there was only the Church of England. There I discovered the literary treasure of the Book of Common Prayer and a glorious theological tradition that cherished the human faculty of reason. But this coexisted with an astonishing biblical illiteracy. Our cultural clashes swirl between bastions of these two shaky poles. The pious quote isolated teachings, stripping them from the nuance in which they are always, always embedded. And "reasoned" liberal or secular analysis of the Bible can dismiss the relevance and mystery of the text with a spirit as literalistic as any fundamentalist stance. A longing to bridge this gap in myself—to know what it meant to revere sacred text and practice and to plumb its insights intellectually as well as spiritually—led me from England to Yale Divinity School in 1991.

My teacher of the New Testament there was an eminently brilliant and wise scholar named Leander Keck. He was in his seventies when I enrolled in his Introduction to New Testament and in his final semesters of teaching. He had been a leader in New Testament scholarship for many decades. He had laid out and picked over every nuance, difference, and discrepancy in the Christian canon and followed the unfolding of archaeological, sociological, and literary documentation of how this collection of writings had come to be over vast periods of time. From Keck I learned that nearly four hundred years passed between the life of Jesus of Nazareth and the collation of the anthology we now call the New Testament. In that period, hundreds of gospels, sayings, and interpretations of Jesus circulated in and between Christian communities as their faith spread like wildfire across the ancient world. The canon—an anthology of texts to set the parameters of orthodoxy—was ultimately closed at the North African Council of Carthage in the year 397. The books that made it into the Bible contained contradictions and open spaces and tensions. Church fathers were alert to these. They scrutinized, debated, and opted to preserve them. With some reluctance they included the Gnostic-tinged Gospel of John and the controversial apocalyptic vision of Revelation.

I have found this basic history to be essential in navigating the biblical headlines of our time—scholarly, cinematic, and otherwise. The perspective Keck imparted to me is traditional, old-fashioned perhaps, and yet deeply learned and essential context for understanding what has passed for "news" these last years: the Jesus Seminar's subjectively stripped-down New Testament; the dizzying mix of fact and fiction in Dan Brown's *Da Vinci Code;* and hyped-up discoveries of Gnostic and other noncanonical gospels. These are not uninteresting or unimportant developments, but we cannot use them wisely without an elementary sense of the tradition they would critique or enhance. Most of us did not get this in church, even if like me we were surrounded by sayings from the Bible.

Leander Keck urged me to read the text as a whole and see it in its complexity. He trained me to discern and honor recurring themes, and also to take different versions of the same story as occasions for finding layers of meaning. In a canon with four Gospels that resisted pressure to synthesize and simplify, he found tremendous depth and freedom and unfolding possibilities for the reader in every generation: the Gospel of Mark's raw confusion and amazement; Matthew's didactic, rabbinically toned diplomacy; John's mysticism and emotion; Luke's Greek-infused semihistorical narratives. The New Testament epistles likewise range in tone and purpose, often contradicting each other. They constituted one side of what was clearly a lively, urgent, and at times tortured correspondence about the struggles of the fledgling church and its fledgling leaders.

And Jesus himself speaks throughout the text mostly in metaphor, parable, and story. In that oral culture, stories could be remembered and passed on intact. Treatises could not. But these stories were not, as they might appear on the surface to a modern eye, child's play. Parables mirror the love of ideas in the Jewish tradition that was Jesus' intellectual and spiritual world of reference—a rich, creative, careful attention to the many meanings words can convey, the many meanings the same words can take in different lives and in the same life over the course of time. Jesus' teachings made room for and honored the differences in his listeners, the varieties of ears and hearts that would apprehend his stories. But deep down they were more challenging than straightforward. The biblical text honestly recounts that Jesus' own hand-picked disciples—clay-footed and beloved like Jacob—often failed to comprehend what he was trying to teach them.

These stories allowed me to live at once more patiently and more expectantly, to accept reality as both messy and mysterious. Jesus' parables, for example, often concern the kingdom of heaven. He describes this to his disciples variously, metaphorically, and to their ears cryptically. It is like yeast, he says, like a hidden treasure, like a mustard seed. In Sunday school, this was presented to me as a straightforward lesson that affirmed the American Dream: great things come of small beginnings. But as I delved into its nuance in a scholarly way, I found a recurrent allusion not merely to the smallness of the seed or the yeast, but also to its hiddenness. The intrinsic puzzle of the kingdom of heaven is the organic mystery that every farmer sees enacted in every harvest season—a minuscule, buried substance holds a wondrous power of transformation and growth within itself.

And here is the conundrum for a results-oriented, American can-do mentality: the only control the planter has is in the act of planting. This reminded me of a teaching of the monk and writer Thomas Merton that I'd puzzled over in England. Merton described the difference between pure intentions and intentions that are merely good or right. These might be the best of intentions—like my habitual longing to save the world. But pure intentions hold realism and mystery in an enlivening tension. Pure intention, as I now understood it, would sanctify what Americans might regard as thankless tasks, limited life-giving work of care as opposed to grand ambitious projects. It is an acknowledgment that sometimes in this world the best you can do is plant the seed, attend patiently and reverently to a reality you cannot change quickly or even in your lifetime, be present to suffering you cannot banish. To summon the kingdom of heaven as Jesus described it is not to call down perfection on an imperfect world, but to bring recurring, overriding virtues of the Gospel—love, mercy, and redemption—to moments that will probably not make headlines.

When *The Da Vinci Code* took the publishing world by storm, I interviewed Luke Timothy Johnson, whose classic textbook, *The Writings of the New Testament,* Leander Keck had assigned us. The thrill of *The Da Vinci Code* was its suggestion of a sexual relationship between Jesus and Mary Magdalene. Our entire culture, after all, not merely its conservative religious, is fixated on private sexual behavior. That novel also quoted from noncanonical gospels that have never been secret, though again few of us heard about them in Sunday school. And the suggestion in *The Da Vinci Code* and other revelations of other texts in recent years has been that they might complete or correct our basic understanding of Christianity. They might be superior for private reading and edification. Luke Timothy Johnson puts this in helpful perspective. The canonical texts, as he tells it, were chosen over others after nearly four centuries of being passed around in early Christian communities because they stood the test of time and *communal practice.* The biblical texts were not meant primarily for private inspiration and contemplation, nor were they designed to be posted on walls or billboards or quoted in debates. They survived because they described a way of life, in community, thought to mirror that of Jesus of Nazareth and the earliest Christians. Our cultural debates about the New Testament by way of movies, books, and popular scholarship focus almost exclusively on the historicity and factuality of aspects of the biblical story. But the essential knowledge they describe has only ever made sense—and become authoritative—when it is lived and embodied. Johnson uses evocative language to describe how he came to understand this in several years he spent early in life as a Benedictine monk:

> As a monk, we sang the psalms and read scripture out loud, five hours a day. So when I went to Yale to get a Ph.D. in New Testament, I was stunned by the academization of all of this and especially by the privileging of history—as if somehow, if we could get the history right, then everything would be okay. . . . And that was quite a contrast from living within, in fact, a living tradition in which scripture was almost kinetically inhabited. You bowed and scraped and genuflected and sang scripture. The notion of

scripture as being a cadaver that one performs an autopsy on—as opposed to a living body with which one danced—was stunning to me. And I never have completely bought it. I have never bought the premise of modernity that history is the only way of knowing.

Ways of knowing. In our time we are again entangled in a clash that takes its passion from the beginning of the beginning of the Bible—the ostensible incompatibility between the Genesis account of creation and the science of evolution. But there is no better example than Genesis of how reading sacred text more seriously, more carefully, not less so, is the surest, strongest antidote to our polarized religio-cultural debates. The irony of this debate, in my mind, is that some of the faithful have fought science on its terms, co-opting and aping its approach to knowledge. In the process they themselves—and our culture at large—have lost sight of the distinctive nature of *scientia sacra,* the nature and content of sacred knowledge. This is a term the Muslim scientist/scholar Seyyed Hossein Nasr likes to use to speak about the poetic, embodied, intuitive way in which sacred traditions point at truth that gives coherence to all of life.

At Yale I also had a wonderful teacher of the Hebrew Bible, or the Christian Old Testament, named Ellen Davis. She introduced me to a recent translation by Everett Fox, *The Five Books of Moses*, that makes the evocative imagery and lyricism of the original Hebrew more transparent in English. We use this translation whenever we can in readings on my radio program, *Speaking of Faith*. Like much of the Hebrew Bible that English translations have straightened into prose on the written page, Genesis 1 is poetic rather than polemic. Just seeing it this way influences the way one hears and internalizes the knowledge it intends to convey. It begins:

> *At the beginning of God's creating*
> *of the heaven and the earth*
> *when the earth was wild and waste,*
> *darkness over the face of Ocean,*
> *Rushing-spirit of God hovering over*
>   *the face of the waters—*
> *God said: Let there be light! And there was light.*
> *God saw the light: that it was good.*
> *God separated the light from the darkness.*
> *God called the light: Day! And the darkness he*
>   *called: Night!*
> *There was setting, there was dawning: one day.*

God proceeds to bring forth the heavens and the oceans and dry land, the plants of the earth, the sun, moon, and stars, the fish of the sea and the birds of the air and creatures of the land. The sun and the moon are out of place in the created order, but everything else in this text is remarkably consonant with the insights of modern geology and genetics. And then on the sixth day, God creates male and female equal and all at once in a mysterious, divine first-person plural voice: "Let us make man in *our* image, after *our* likeness . . . so God created man in his own image, in the image of God he created him; *male and female he created them.*"

This is a text with a purpose, but that purpose has nothing to do with refuting science. It is meant to posit that God created the heavens and the earth—and that the sun is part of this creation, not its apex and origin as earlier societies believed. The sun is put in its place here, not the human capacity to explore and explain the inner workings of the natural world. For centuries, until the medieval period and the Reformation, the great Christian theologians knew this and honored it. To treat this text as a commentary on science is to ignore its textual intention and coherence, just as to read a poem as prose is to miss the point.

In fact in this first chapter of Genesis that posits God's days of creation, there is no Eden, no Adam, no Eve, no original sin, no fall. Those characters and themes received an almost exclusive focus in the Sunday schools of my childhood. But Adam and Eve only first appear in the second chapter of Genesis, where a separate and quite different creation story picks up, narrated in a markedly different voice and with a different set of literary purposes. This also has nothing to do with science. It is a morality tale, a reflection on the patterns of the human heart. Genesis 2 is at once a tale of beginnings and a drama eternally reenacted. In Hebrew, Eden means "delight." It is a place where out of the ground the Lord God grew every tree that was "pleasant to the sight" and only secondarily "good for food"; a place where the man and his wife lived as one flesh, naked and content; a place where they occasionally met God walking in the garden in the cool of the day. The tempter—whom we have embellished in popular telling with supernatural status and imagined as Satan—is unambiguously part of the natural world, a serpent, and just that. There is no apple in the story, only a piece of fruit. And Eve is not fashioned from Adam's "rib," but from his "side." These are minor details, perhaps, but telling examples of how we insert interpretations and images onto texts we know well, to the extent that we may ultimately not know them at all.

As a child, I read Eden's drama of creation and fall as prescriptive: a tale that turns on bad behavior and has a predictable sorry ending. But as I revisit these texts as an adult, I hear them as perceptively descriptive. The narrators of Eden named and pondered the fact that something was terribly at odds with the way life should fundamentally be and they wondered about the roots of this ongoing reality. The bringing forth of life was a painful and dangerous affair. The work that defined men's lives was often not a pleasure but a chore. The pattern even in this world's most intimate relationship was one of domination. And the world had a habit of being beguiled by distractions within its own delightfulness. The serpent that beguiled Eve, the text says, was "crafty." In the Hebrew, this word is unmistakably akin to the "nakedness" of which Adam and Eve were originally unashamed. Cleverness and innocence were both blessings here, both gifts, not definitively incompatible, yet when corrupted at odds. God gave Adam and Eve the entire garden to enjoy, including the Tree of Life at its center. God forbade them only to eat of the fruit of the Tree of the Knowledge of Good and Evil.

For many years I, a lover of knowledge (especially knowledge about good and evil) balked like the serpent at this puzzling ban. I commiserated with Eve, who transgressed God's command and clandestinely ate; I sympathized with Adam, who ate too when he saw that she did not perish as a result. But the knowledge Adam and Eve gained from eating the forbidden fruit was inconsequential knowledge, evil in petty forms as evil usually comes. They suddenly knew that they were naked, knew shame, knew to lie and to blame each other and to fear. They knew to hide from God, who still came walking toward them in the cool of the day. Bonhoeffer looked inside the Hebrew describing the forbidden knowledge of good and evil, and offered this haunting interpretation of the meaning of this story that all of theology explores:

> Good and Evil, *tob* and *ra*, here have a much wider meaning than *good* and *evil* in our terminology. The words *tob* and *ra* speak of an ultimate division in the world of man in general which goes beyond moral discord, so that *tob* would perhaps also mean "full of pleasure" and *ra* "full of pain." *Tob* and *ra* are the categories for the deepest division of human life in every aspect. The essential thing about them is that they appear as a pair and that, in their state of division, they belong inseparably together.

Such is the knowledge that scripture ponders and describes: the createdness of the world is posited, yes, but a world freed to experience and self-creation; a world imparted in the image of God and with the freedom of God; a world of accomplishment and conflict intertwined, of pleasure and pain that both haunt and enliven each other at the depths of human experience.

In Christianity alone among the major religious traditions, sharp battle lines have been drawn since the Enlightenment between the content of knowledge that religion describes and the form of knowledge that science pursues. The extremes of both positions are intolerant toward the very notion of the other worldview. They calcify into political modes of ideology and combative certainty. They collapse the sense of mystery that is as alive at the heart of science as of religion, two kindred never-ending pursuits of revelation and discovery.

But in the vast middle of our vigorously spiritual modern culture, scientific and religious truths coexist and intertwine for the most part peaceably. We all encounter and respond to the fruits of science in our doctors' offices, through experiences of birth, illness, and death, in the ever-evolving technology at the center of everyday life. Opinion polls promote false dichotomies. Ask Americans to choose between God and Darwin and they'll opt for God. But generations of Christian Americans have also grown up learning about evolution in scientific textbooks and about a God be-hind creation in church—and intuitively reconciling them, instinctively imagining that both might simultaneously be true. What has changed in our time is that a new generation is being actively taught to see discord between them.

One of the great joys of my life of religious conversation has been in speaking with scientists themselves from many disciplines. These conversations teach me that the insights of science and of theology are complementary disciplines that can mutually enrich and illuminate the deepest ques-tions and frontiers of human life and of faith.

Scientists embody a *delving spirit*—the same kind of driving and insatiable curiosity that the psychiatrist Robert Coles has described in children's innate kinship with the original "spirit of religion." They carry it into adulthood and apply it to the cosmos, the natural world, the human body. And from a theological standpoint, if one takes seriously the notion of God as creator, doesn't that make God the original physicist and biologist, geologist and astronomer? Until very recently in historical terms—a few centuries ago—the clas-sic Western scientists lived a version of that idea. Even when they struggled with the church, Copernicus, Galileo, and Newton believed that their discoveries would widen human comprehension of the nature of God. The more we could understand about the world around us in all its intricacy, this reasoning went, the better we would understand the mind of its maker. Charles Darwin followed in this tradition. Here again, I have found remembering forward a refreshing antidote to our cultural debates. In a fuller memory of Darwin, the world he analyzed, and the religious implications of his work, I discern new conversation points for an old misunderstanding.

A passionate amateur naturalist, the son of a physician father and a devout Unitarian mother, the young Darwin was headed for a career in the church. But first he seized a chance to travel on the five-year journey of the HMS *Beagle*. The *Beagle* took him to the southernmost tip of South America. He waited twenty years to publish the theories he began to develop there, painfully aware of the worldview he would unsettle. Darwin's *Origin of Species* was the last classic scientific text to engage theology directly, not the first to dismiss it. He anticipated religious questions and objections at every turn and responded carefully to them. He did not shy from the word *creation*—he used it copiously—but he understood it as an unfolding reality. Once set in motion, as he came to see it, the laws of nature sustained a self-organizing progression driven by the needs and struggles of the natural world itself. The word *reverence* would not be too strong for the attitude with which Darwin approached all he saw in the natural world. There is a great intellectual and spiritual passion, and a touching sense of wonder, evident in his published works as in his private journals and correspondence. In his field notebook in Bahia, Brazil, just before Easter Sunday of 1832, there is this near-poetry: "twiners entwining twiners—tresses like hair—beautiful lepidoptera—Silence—hosannah—" In his *Beagle Diary*, of the view from the summit of an Andean peak, he wrote this:

> When we reached the crest & looked backwards, a glorious view was presented. The atmosphere so resplendently clear, the sky an intense blue, the profound valleys, the wild broken forms, the heaps of ruins piled up during the lapse of ages, the bright colored rocks, contrasted with the quiet mountains of Snow, together produced a scene I never could have imagined. Neither plant or bird, excepting a few condors wheeling around the higher pinnacles, distracted the attention from the inanimate mass.—I felt glad I was by myself, it was like watching a thunderstorm, or hearing in the full Orchestra a Chorus of the Messiah.

And at the end of his journey in September 1836, Darwin reflected on all he had seen with words that defy the rift that his scientific conclusions would set in motion:

> Among the scenes which are deeply impressed on my mind, none exceed in sublimity the primeval forests, undefaced by the hand of man, whether those of Brazil, where the powers of life are predominant, or those of Tierra del Fuego, where death & decay prevail. Both are temples filled with the varied productions of the God of Nature:—No one can stand unmoved in these solitudes, without feeling that there is more in man than the mere breath of his body.

Darwin used the biblically evocative analogy of the "tree of life"—the tree from which Adam and Eve were free to eat in the center of the garden of Eden—to illustrate his theory of natural selection. He drew species sprouting like branches from the same trunk, some flourishing and others withering and falling to nourish the ground in which the whole is sustained. His vision of all of life netted together is profoundly consonant with what we are learning now in environmental sciences as well as genetics. It is consonant with old and new impulses across the world's spiritual traditions, from paganism to evangelical Christianity, to take an active and responsible part in honoring the diversity of natural life and sustaining its connections.

Approaching Darwin with fresh eyes and new questions, I am also struck by the theological and moral implications his science held—the new vision of the nature of God and human life that it made possible. He grew up in the rarified world of Jane Austen's novels. That social habitat was held by Christian England to be divinely ordained—conceived all at once at the beginning of time. It should be, like every condition of plant and animal, fixed and static and eternal. But in South America, the young Darwin saw a flourishing slave trade as well as desperate conditions of life that defied every standard of the genteel world in which he was raised. In Chile, where he first saw fossil layers unearthed, he also contemplated immense devastation that reflected the essence of nature as surely as beauty. He returned to an English society instituting workhouses and debtors' prisons to hold social chaos at bay. Religious thinkers in his age were busily formulating a theology to correspond—an image of God who instituted poverty and misery as the price for sloth and vice. And in some sense, in documenting the freedom of the physical world to define its own fruitfulness in and through chaos and struggle—to progress through the interplay between *tob* and *ra*—Darwin liberated God from the minute details of this chaos and struggle. He liberated humanity from belief in a God who designed and enacted every flaw, every catastrophe, every inborn injustice within nature and human society.

As his biographer James Moore put it to me, Darwin forced human beings to look at the inherent struggle of life head-on, not as we wish it to be, but as it is in all its complexity, brutality, and mystery. "He brings you up short," Moore says, "bang against the world as it really is in his vision, not the world that we would like it to be, as if there hadn't been a fall into sin in the Garden of Eden." This hard grasp of reality is most taxing for human beings, perhaps, in times of great change and turmoil. Tides of resistance to Darwin's ideas have peaked in periods of cultural flux and global danger and human fearfulness. The Scopes Monkey Trial took place between two world wars and as the U.S. economy moved toward depression.

I'm disposed to look for the intriguing middle ground where science and religion interact because I stumbled upon it as I was first beginning to approach large spiritual questions again in adulthood. As a child of the Enlightenment, the problem of needless and wanton suffering in the world stood in the way of my giving in completely to faith. There is no proving that God exists. But the magnitude of suffering in the world is the most logical of arguments against that notion. This is the high religious territory of theodicy, the problem of evil. Why the interplay of *tob* and *ra,* pleasure and pain, in human life to begin with? Why the brutality of nature that Darwin described alongside its beauty? If the creator is an uninvolved intelligence that abandoned us to hazardous laws of nature and human behavior, what is the point of an involved faith on our part? More dispassionately, if creation is a double-edged sword, then perhaps the concept of God is beyond comprehension in space and time. And that is where Darwin and many scientists and other moderns, understandably, have been content to leave him.

The German philosopher Gottfried Leibniz coined the term *theodicy*—from the Greek, meaning "the justice of God"—in 1710. He argued that evil in the world does not disprove or minimize the essential goodness of God's creation, which would always outweigh the bad. Despite the reality of suffering, he proclaimed, this is "the best of all possible worlds." But then in 1755 one of the deadliest earthquakes in history hit the city of Lisbon at 10:35 on the morning of November 1, All Saints Day. Something like thirty thousand people died in the first six minutes alone, many of them crushed in midliturgy under the collapsed roofs of packed churches. It was difficult in this case to resurrect the theory, floated previously, that earthquakes and other natural disasters reflected the wrath of God on sinful people and nations. In fact, it was easy, even supremely logical, for the French philosopher Voltaire to ask, How can this possibly be the best of all worlds? In the face of such evidence, how can any rational person believe in a benevolent creator God? Theodicy came to be the trump card that threw the entire religious enterprise into doubt.

I suspect that we have all posed the theodicy question in our lives. Even those of us who are not religious have felt it press on our longing for the world just to make sense. Just as I came back to take religion seriously in 1989, the large-scale geopolitical suffering that had gripped me for years disintegrated with mind-boggling rapidity and consequences. On my twenty-ninth birthday, I learned as I stepped off an airplane that the Berlin Wall had opened up. Communist East Germany soon vanished. The truths and texts of that time—the nuclear arms agreements I watched in the making, our obsessive Cold War faith in the might of the Soviet Union, the Berlin Wall my friends and I bewailed as a permanent fixture of history—these things shockingly, abruptly, ceased to matter. The human spirit eventually defies the best-laid plans of politics, and we can guess so little of the history before us. Surprise is a staple of my theology—one of the threads I find woven into the texture of life—in part because of this history I've lived through.

Still, as euphoria dispersed and change penetrated in the year after the Wall came down, I began hearing story after story from friends about how hard newfound freedom could be on human personality and relationships. Suffering never quite went away, it seemed, it simply moved around. It was a shape shifter. Now I inhabited a small English village of quiet lives and relatively contained problems, but there were still manifold ways for people to find themselves and others desperately unhappy—that divorce, this illness, that drinking problem, this obstinate personality that could translate unwittingly into everyday evil. Human pain was more transparent in this place, not less so, not obscured by geopolitical destiny. I was in the throes of a happy early marriage, but back at home my parents were divorcing and I was estranged from them both. New hurts seemed to rush in on me and others I loved even as one dilemma achieved a peaceful solution, like a well that constantly renews itself, as vigorous at least as the well of joy.

At the beginning of my theological musings in Codford St. Mary, I discovered two lines of thought that made some sense and have guided and framed my understanding ever since. They insisted that I look at the hard edges of reality and ask religion to make sense there.

The first was in a slim book that has never become famous, written by an English medieval historian named Margaret Spufford. It had the apt and ironic title *Celebration*. Spufford's life has been marked with great misfortune—the stuff theologians call "natural evil," evil perpetrated by organic processes and properties of nature itself. After bearing and nursing two children, she learned that these maternal imperatives had accelerated an extreme form of early onset osteoporosis. She would spend much of the rest of her life severely limited in movement, often bedridden, with a constant threat of bone fracture and breakage. To add to this, her second child, a daughter, Brigit, was born with a calamitous disease of the blood. She spent her twenty-two years in and out of hospitals. Spufford was an intellectual but not a religiously learned person, simply an Anglican layperson who developed a religious curiosity and a contemplative bent and began to read and pray, think and write. Her personal suffering has been the equivalent of a genetic earthquake. She has pondered the beloved, gorgeous lines of Psalm 139, with a life that does not bear out its comforting lines: "You formed my inward parts, you knit me together in my mother's womb; I praise you, for I am fearfully and wonderfully made." Did God, she had to ask, preordain her treacherously weakened bones? Did God design and switch on the genetic malfunction that turned her daughter's short life into one episode of suffering after the next? And what about all of these promises, in the same prayer book of the Bible, the Psalms, that God will "rescue the faithful," "hide them under the shadow of his wings"?

Margaret Spufford concludes—in the way of many profound religious insights—that such questions must be reframed if we are to approach anything like an answer. She cannot resolve the dilemma of her daughter's apparently "flawed" creation or her own. That remains in the territory of mystery. She had, rather, a cathartic and visceral certainty that God is present in the suffering with them. Spufford carries the teachings of the Sunday schools of my childhood—of Jesus suffering for our sake, even to the point of feeling abandoned by God as he hung on the cross—to a new kind of meaning. The center of Christianity holds an astonishing premise of a creator/author God who entered the confines and hazards of the story of life once it was set in motion—a God who threw himself whole into space and time, the light and the darkness of life, with us. The goodness of God, Spufford came to believe, does not banish the suffering that is bafflingly rife in this world, but shares it. This became for her a plausible way to faith. "To the knowledge of the incarnation," she writes, "not to the image of an omnipotent creator, I have clung like a limpet. On those terrible children's wards I could neither have worshipped nor respected any God who had not himself cried, 'My God, my God, why hast thou forsaken me?'"

My second epiphany in thinking about suffering and reality and the leap of faith came late one Saturday night on the BBC with an essay by a scientist—the quantum physicist John Polkinghorne. In Polkinghorne's descriptions of the world physicists know, I began to hear a cosmic extension of the morality tale of Genesis. Every minute aspect of this living world, he said, has free will—not just human hearts and minds, but animals and plants, storm clouds, cancer cells, tectonic plates. This sets up a constant jostling, competition, and collision between strong given natures, an inevitable shadow side to creation. There is suffering, and there are losers, and there is muddle. But Polkinghorne adds that quantum physics, as it has evolved, is describing something more "supple" and "subtle" than a world merely left to the relentless inertia of natural laws. It sees a backdrop of interplay between order and disorder, between patterned structure and open possibilities. Multitudinous life functions in its essence and moves forward relentlessly—human beings breathe; grass grows; storm clouds gather. But there are also places of randomness, openings in fixed processes, that might have implications for something like prayer. The laws of nature make room for human action and possibly also for God to act in time and space.

Fifteen years and a changed life later, I sit with John Polkinghorne in a radio studio in St. Paul. In midlife, John Polkinghorne became a theologian and an Anglican priest. He creatively employs his knowledge as a scientist as he makes sense of the world and of religion. He says, for example,

> Well, certainly God is not a god in a hurry. That's clear. God is patient and subtle. God works through process and not through magic; not through snapping the divine fingers. And I think that's what we learn from seeing the history of creation as science has revealed it. And I think that tells us something about how God acts generally. And, when you think about it, if God really is a god whose nature is best described as being the God of love, then that is how love will work. Not by overwhelming force, but by, if you like, persuasive process. So I think we learn something really quite valuable from that. Again, it's an example of how religious

insights about the nature of God and the scientific insights about the process of the world seem to me actually to be very consonant with each other. You can't deduce one from the other, but you can see it and they fit together in a way that makes sense. They don't seem to be at odds with each other, and I find that encouraging.

Both science and religion are needed, Polkinghorne has written, "to interpret and understand the rich, varied and surprising way the world actually is." He says to me, of the different forms of knowledge that science and religion convey,

Science treats the world as an object, something you could put to the test, pull apart and find out what it's made of. And, of course, that's a very interesting thing to do, and you learn some important things that way. But we know that there are whole realms of human experience where first of all testing has to give way to trusting. That's true in human relationships. If I'm always setting little traps to see if you're my friend, I'll destroy the possibility of friendship between us. And also where we have to treat things in their wholeness, in their totality. I mean, a beautiful painting, a chemist could take that beautiful painting, could analyze every scrap of paint on the canvas, tell you what its chemical composition was, would incidentally destroy the painting by doing that, but would have missed the point of the painting, because that's something you can only encounter in its totality. So we need complementary ways of looking at the world.

Ways of looking. The most compelling illustration I know of this world of astonishing, seething, colliding wills that science describes I find in a work of fiction, *The Poisonwood Bible,* by the naturalist/novelist Barbara Kingsolver. Kingsolver paints a compelling picture, by way of art and story, of converging territory between scientific and theological observation. In this passage I have marked up and returned to time and again, Adah Price, daughter of missionaries, returns to Africa after studying medicine and sees God and the world of nature with new metaphors, new eyes.

What human beings experience as natural evil is here conveyed as an expression of divine reverence for the diversity of natures and wills that drive creation forward. It is posited as vivid and generous if confusing evidence of that enduring principle of the religion of my childhood, of divine belovedness for all of life:

> As a teenager reading African parasitology books in the medical library, I was boggled by the array of creatures equipped to take root upon a human body. I'm boggled still, but with a finer appreciation for the partnership. Back then I was still a bit appalled that God would set down his barefoot boy and girl dollies into an Eden where, presumably, He had just turned loose elephantiasis and microbes that eat the human cornea. Now I understand, God is not just rooting for the dollies. We and our vermin all blossomed together out of the same humid soil in the Great Rift Valley, and so far no one is really winning. Five million years is a long partnership. If you could for a moment rise up out of your own beloved skin and ap-

praise ant, human and virus as equally re-
sourceful beings, you might admire the
accord they have all struck in Africa.

Now I know that even as episodes of religious hostility to
science make headlines in this country, there is a lively inter-
face between religious thinkers and scientists across many
traditions, globally, and in many fields—astronomy, com-
puter science, biology, physics, genetics. Beyond our culture's
entrenched debates, a parallel universe of dialogue is unfolding. Things in this universe confound and transcend the narrow imagination of our culture wars. There are points of
disagreement, to be sure, and contrasting perspectives and
areas where the conversation stops. But blinders off, defenses
down, I see that scientists—especially those who work with
mathematics—possess a reverence for beauty as strong as
their reverence for reason. If an equation is not elegant and
beautiful, they will tell you as a solemn point of fact, it is
likely not true. Science's theoreticians are as likely to employ
analogy and metaphor as poets or mystics. They routinely
proceed to new heights of knowledge by way of faith in
things unseen.

Images and ideas from the world of science repeatedly
give me new, creative ways to think about the "rationality" of

religious modes of thought. The wildly imaginative discipline of physics alone is rife with pointers. Contemporary physics revolves around objects, premises—quarks, for example, and strings—that no one has ever seen or expects to "see"; but worlds of passion and discovery and progress thrive on them, because the idea of them gives intelligibility to the whole of what can be measured and experienced and observed. Or consider this: a scientific puzzle that Einstein chewed on, the question of whether light is a particle or a wave, was resolved by a teacher of John Polkinghorne, Paul Dirac, with the unexpected, seemingly illogical conclusion that it is both. And here's the key that made that discovery possible: how we ask our questions affects the answers we arrive at. Light appears as a wave if you ask it "a wavelike question" and it appears as a particle if you ask it "a particle-like question." This is a wonderful template for understanding how contradictory explanations of reality can simultaneously be true.

Science like religion is about questions more than answers—questions and more questions that meet every new answer as soon as it is hatched. It's not so much true that science and religion reach different answers on the same questions of human life, which is how our cultural debate has defined the rift between them. Far more often, they simply ask different kinds of questions altogether, and the responses they generate together illuminate human life more completely than either could do alone. The biologist Carl Feit of Yeshiva University helped me understand this first. He describes his clinical pursuit of cancer and his religious study of the Talmud as dual intellectual quests. Science asks penetrating questions of "how." Tools of science can even illuminate properties and processes of what we identify as good and evil. But science is neither innately concerned nor equipped to pose questions of "why" or "what next" in a moral, spiritual, or existential sense. Feit says,

> The physical universe doesn't come beset with values. It's kind of neutral in the sense that it can be used for good and for bad. From the scientific perspective, everything that we can discover we should discover. The problem comes up, what do you do with something once you've discovered it? That was the moral dilemma faced by the scientists after World War II . . . when they realized that they were working on exploring and exploiting the potential energy that's present in an atom. That's a two-edged sword that could be used to destroy humanity. But

it also can be used to cure cancer. We use radionuclides in our treatment of cancer.

So from the scientific point of view, Feit says, you've made a discovery. He turns to religious tradition as the richest repository he has for asking, what's going to happen with that discovery? And how will it be used with human beings?

I have also loved several conversations I've had with the geneticist Lyndon Eaves. He is a professor in both human genetics and psychiatry at the Virginia Commonwealth University School of Medicine and the principal investigator on some of the nation's largest ongoing long-term studies of twins. Outside the laboratory, he is also an Episcopal priest. He is a passionate scientist—in a way scientists often are, I find, as exuberant as any artist. He loves his art of genetics and is nearly obsessed by its infinite possibilities, by the intriguing boundaries of human knowledge that he has helped push to new places. But he is clear-eyed at the same time about the limits of science, the questions it can't and doesn't aspire to ask—and the human drama he encounters outside the laboratory that his data can't encompass. We're all living "a life of experiment," Eaves says, in every aspect of our experience. And he cautions that even the best answers of science and religion can become idols, blocking our view of the complexity of what it means to be human.

The new frontiers of Darwin's notion of "natural selection" are in Eaves's field of genetics and disciplines like neurology—fields of research on which new generations of scientists are mapping out the biological roots of human survival and adaptation. There are theories that religion itself arose and survived because it had evolutionary value. There is a whole field called neurotheology. The mind-body connection that Buddhism has cultivated for thousands of years has become scientifically observable. Spiritual experiences can be mapped physiologically by brain imaging technology. This raises the question of whether human spirituality is generated by the brain, rather than by a transcendent maker. On the other hand, some counter, wouldn't the mind behind life instill a capacity in human beings to apprehend it and communicate? Or are our most debased and transcendent instincts driven by a "selfish gene," or a "God gene"? I'm fascinated by how uninterested Lyndon Eaves is in these emerging debates and their bantering either-or choices. He proposes another set of questions and concerns altogether:

> Clearly, there's a big investment in some people's minds in genes that are of socioeconomic value—genes that influence IQ, genes that influence income. And there have

been papers around all of those, which may be true, and then have purported to infer more conservative and, let's say, restricting options for humanity on the basis of that. I also would love to find the genes that whenever we listen to something like that make us want to cry, "Bullshit." You know, where are the genes that give us the passion for justice, the passion for looking for something beyond the current restriction? Where are the genes that make us transcend those limitations and fight against them?

What we currently choose to study about the human, Lyndon Eaves feels, is a "pretty pathetic subset" of what it is to be human.

You can choose to define your anthropology in terms of what, for example, psychologists think we can measure, or we can choose to define anthropology in terms of all the things that people write novels about and write poems about and write music for. How do you get from something as simple as

DNA and complex as the world outside and other people to what we understand quintessentially as the person? I think that's where the real challenge, the real fascination comes.

The Jewish bioethicist Laurie Zoloth is working at the furthest reaches of reproductive technologies. As she does so, she also works with the Talmud, and with biblical texts, that have carried ancient stories and conversations into the present. The rabbinical legend of the golem, for example, is a centuries-old reflection on what it would mean to create a human being. It is a fable on the limits of human wisdom and power, and it has been picked up as a way to reflect on life in our time by writers like Cynthia Ozick, Elie Wiesel, and Marge Piercy. The golems and their creators always go astray, as Laurie Zoloth tells it, in "the unhitching of the man from morality." She finds these kinds of religious resources growing more relevant in modernity, not less so. For example, she says,

Here I am in the twenty-first century, wandering down the lab, down the next building, and looking at the actual machine that can pull apart the cells and thinking about this. And then going back and hauling out my volumes of the Talmud, you know, and thinking, "What an interesting thing. What an interesting response."

The texts that come to mind for me are the texts of this tradition, the Talmudic texts and the arguments, in part because it's a complicated compilation of both law and fantasy and a moral universe constructed with mere story and mere language. Of course, not "mere" at all. But if I'm trying to think about the creation of our own moral universe, and if all we have really is words and language, then the use of story, the use of narrative, becomes quite important again. Because the laws might fail us. The laws are in some ways a rather impartial account of the complicated technology and the complicated possibilities we're faced with. We are faced with what's been called "fiction science," science that's just beyond the borders of our imagination. And at that border I think the use of *midrashic* accounts and stories might be best employed. Because it's such a fantastic idea, we need rather fantastic and metaphorical allusions to think about them.

Yet just as someone like Laurie Zoloth surprises me with her creative allusions and physicists surprise me with their alert and minute reverence for beauty, religious perspectives in this realm often surprise me with a clear-eyed attention to the hard realities of three-dimensional life. Genetics doesn't sit with the hopes, fears, and longing of the patient in the final stages of pancreatic cancer, Lyndon Eaves says. Our culture seeks to deny or to tame the enduring mystery of the beginning of life, the inevitability of death, our ordinary and persistent struggles for meaning in between. But traditions and texts and practices of faith accompany these, grapple with them, sanctify them. The anthropology of faith—its insistence that critical aspects of life are unquantifiable, unsolvable, flawed, and nevertheless blessed—puts it squarely in the camp of reality if not logic. The great traditions are not systems for an impossible perfection but for aspiration to grace within the possibilities and the boundaries of every life, every moment.

Dietrich Bonhoeffer read the physics of his day even from the prison where he died, and he worried about a stunted religious imagination that would consign God to the borders where scientific knowledge gives out. A sentence that struck me from my earliest readings of Bonhoeffer comes back now with new connotations: "I worry that Christians who have only one foot on earth can also only have one foot in heaven." He concluded from the depths of a man-made darkness—in words rich with allusion for me now of Margaret Spufford and John Polkinghorne and many, many others—that "we are to find God in what we know, not in what we don't know; God wants us to realize his presence, not in unsolved problems but in those that are solved. That is true of the relationship between God and scientific knowledge, but it is also true of the wider human problems of death, suffering, and guilt."

Bonhoeffer's friend and nephew-in-law Eberhard Bethge compiled and published his *Letters and Papers from Prison* after his death. They became more famous, and more widely read by people religious and nonreligious, than any of the books he wrote in his lifetime. As I have moved through the world beyond Berlin, I have been astonished to uncover vast networks of unlikely people who converse with Bonhoeffer's ideas and example. The whistle-blowing FBI special agent Coleen Rowley took solace in his theology as she was reviled by her own agency in the wake of the 9/11 attacks that she believes her office might have stopped. The Vietnamese Zen Buddhist monk and poet Thich Nhat Hanh found new hope when he read Bonhoeffer's writings from prison as war consumed his country in the 1960s. He forsook monastic isolation to organize efforts for victims of that war and to work for reconciliation among all the warring parties. He led the Buddhist delegation to the 1969 Paris peace talks. Bonhoeffer inspired his "engaged Buddhism," he says, and kept him going.

With difficulty, I begin to understand this: in death, and in the power of his ideas beyond his death, Bonhoeffer may have borne perfect witness to his understanding of God—a God science may help us imagine more richly and completely. Bonhoeffer succumbed to Hitler's terror, but he was not lost to time, and he was not lost to love. In this theology, the darkness is made light because God too is dying, and rising again, in slums, prisons, wars, mudslides, and earthquakes, within and despite our accidents and our frailty as well as our cruelty.

I spoke with the Columbia biologist Robert Pollack after the 9/11 terrorist attacks. He points out that human beings become capable of otherwise unthinkable acts against one another—torture, murder, and a logic of loathing entire races and peoples—when they convince themselves that those others are less than human. In this sense, Pollack says, moral evil caused by human will and action mirrors natural evil. The human enemy becomes expendable when he can be approached as an inferior life form in the way of our dominance or survival. This was an impulse rampant in hundreds of years of colonialism, where racial prejudice fed illusions not just of cultural but of biological superiority. It was at work when my forebears settled Oklahoma out from under native peoples who had walked the Trail of Tears to get there. Tutsis were no longer neighbors but "cockroaches" to Hutus. The people in those airplanes on 9/11 were not parents and siblings and children but symbols, and ammunition, for the young Saudis who crashed them into the twin towers and the Pentagon and the Pennsylvania earth. Pollack finds understanding in this analogy that he draws from biology, as do I, but not peace of mind. For that, he says, he turns to the prayers of Jewish piety that sanctify the mundane and cruel realities of life moment to moment. That, he says, is not enough, and at the same time it is more than enough. As a scientist as well as a religious man, he lives with mystery and understanding both.

I think of Bob Pollack when I am finally able to interview Elie Wiesel two decades after our first meeting in Berlin. I want to speak with Wiesel this time about God, though for years after I began to pursue religious questions and ideas, I had heard Wiesel described as an icon of the loss of faith. I could never quite accept that as the whole story, especially after he began to publish volumes of Hasidic tales in more recent years. I sit across from him in a hotel room that my producers have turned into a makeshift studio. He is grace personified.

Elie Wiesel tells me that he holds human beings responsible for the evil of Auschwitz and Birkenau, not God. "God gives us the world which he wanted—not perfect but beautiful. And what are we doing to it?" He cites an idea first described by the Jewish philosopher Martin Buber, that in certain historical periods there is an "eclipse of God." Perhaps, he imagines, the Holocaust was so massive and unbearable that God turned his face away. Still, he cannot help but be angry with God for that. This anger was born in his childhood and smolders today. I ask Elie Wiesel if he will read aloud a passage of *Night*, which is often quoted as proof of the illegitimacy of faith amid the modern world and its horrors. He hands the book back and asks me to read it instead. It is absurd that I should read these words to this man. But I do.

> Never shall I forget that night, the first night
> in camp, which has turned my life into one
> long night, seven times cursed and seven
> times sealed. Never shall I forget that smoke.
> Never shall I forget the little faces of the chil-

dren, whose bodies I saw turned into wreaths of smoke beneath a silent blue sky.

Never shall I forget those flames which consumed my faith forever.

Never shall I forget that nocturnal silence which deprived me, for all eternity, of the desire to live. Never shall I forget those moments which murdered my God and my soul and turned my dreams to dust. Never shall I forget these things, even if I am condemned to live as long as God Himself. Never.

I close the book and ask Elie Wiesel, What happened after that? What happened after you lost your faith forever?

"What happened after is in the book," he says. "I went on praying." And he proceeds to give me a great gift of words that transcend words. He does not answer the problem of evil. Graciously, helpfully, he translates it into clear-eyed and reality-bound prayer—prayer with room for both questions and answers, anger and mystery.

I no longer ask You for either happiness or paradise; all I ask of You is to listen and let me be aware of Your listening.

I no longer ask You to resolve my questions, only to receive them and make them part of You.

I no longer ask You for either rest or wisdom, I only ask You not to close me to gratitude, be it of the most trivial kind, or to surprise and friendship. Love? Love is not Yours to give.

As for my enemies, I do not ask You to punish them or even to enlighten them; I only ask You not to lend them Your mask and Your powers. If You must relinquish one or the other, give them Your powers. But not Your countenance.

They are modest, my requests, and humble. I ask You what I might ask a stranger met by chance at twilight in a barren land.

I ask You, God of Abraham, Isaac, and Jacob, to enable me to pronounce these words without betraying the child that transmitted them to me: God of Abraham, Isaac, and Jacob, enable me to forgive You and enable the child I once was to forgive me too.

I no longer ask You for the life of that child, nor even for his faith. I only beg You

to listen to him and act in such a way that
You and I can listen to him together.

Albert Einstein fled Berlin as early-twentieth-century German xenophobia and anti-Semitism grew. To his devastation, his esteemed scientific colleagues were not immune. At
an early age, he had disavowed Jewish piety for the reasoned
wonder of geometry and the natural order that science alone
could describe. But when the world of his adulthood fell
short of the order and elegance of mathematics, he became
something of a moral crusader—a facet of his legacy that is
all but forgotten. Einstein used his unusual fame to agitate
for the Jewish people and for political prisoners in fascist
Europe. He later championed the nonviolent resistance of
his contemporary, India's Mahatma Gandhi. Einstein identi-
fied Gandhi, along with other figures such as Jesus, Moses,
St. Francis of Assisi, and Buddha, as spiritual geniuses—
"geniuses in the art of living" more necessary to the sustenance of global human dignity, security, and joy than the
discovery of objective knowledge.

Einstein's grand scientific discoveries had to do with the
evolution of stars and galaxies, with light and gravity, and so
there was less in his science than in Darwin's at which humanity might take offense. But Einstein's laws of physics—
even more than Darwin's laws of nature—were economical

and self-sustaining and could not tolerate a meddling divine hand. Still, Einstein left behind a rich body of reflection on the "mind" and "superior spirit" behind these laws and the cosmos that also never made its way into popular memory. From childhood onward—and Einstein spoke often of childhood wonderings and delvings as a crucible of his life-long curiosity—he thrilled to all he could not yet understand. He was content with what he called his "cosmic religious sense"—animated by "inklings" and "wonderings" more than answers and conclusions. In an address at a conference on science, philosophy, and religion in 1941, Einstein averred that science like religion is created by those who aspire toward truth and understanding. He famously concluded: "Science without religion is lame. Religion without science is blind." In many other musings and addresses he stressed how both realms acknowledge and honor the human sense of mystery:

> The fairest thing we can experience is the mysterious. It is the fundamental emotion which stands at the cradle of true art and true science. He who knows it not and can no longer wonder, no longer feel amazement, is as good as dead. A snuffed-out candle. It was the experience of mystery, even if

mixed with fear, that engendered religion. A knowledge of the existence of something we cannot penetrate, of the manifestations of the profoundest reason and the most radiant beauty—it is this knowledge and this emotion that constitute the truly religious attitude. In this sense, and in this alone, I am a deeply religious man.

After he settled in Princeton in 1933, Einstein saw racism in America as evil, and he condemned segregation with a clarity that eluded most Americans of that time. Having escaped anti-Semitism, he was appalled by this structural injustice in the land of freedom and equality that he had chosen as his home. Not one to mince words, he called it "a disease of white people." S. James Gates Jr., an African American string theorist, describes how stunned he was to learn of this passion of Einstein—long after he launched a career as one of Einstein's scientific inheritors. Gates suggests a fascinating correlation between Einstein's capacity for ethical and social engagement and his scientific creativity. Einstein's most brilliant achievements emerged, as Gates tells it, from penetrating "what-if" questions, which he articulated as "parables" and worked relentlessly to comprehend. For example, Einstein traced his discovery of the theory of relativity back to wondering what would happen to space and time "if he could ride along on a beam of light." Gates believes that this imaginative intellectual approach to such questions inclined Einstein always to question the parameters of reality as given—in other words, to ask "what if" about the condition of human beings as well as the forces of nature, and to acquire the animating ethical virtue of empathy. He seemed able to imagine himself in African American shoes, just as he rode that beam of light toward understanding the very essence of light, energy, and matter from within.

That virtue of empathy fell short in Einstein's personal life, as we now know vividly from correspondence made public since Einstein's death. It was hard to be Einstein's wife, as his biographer Tom Levenson says, and hard to be his child. In researching his fascinating book about Einstein and his time, *Einstein in Berlin,* Levenson wrestled with the complexity of Einstein's humanity, his shadow side. Like other "great" human beings, he finally concludes, the temptation is to idealize Einstein's genius and make him a saint. And while there is no excusing the fact that he hurt people close to him, there is a kind of solace as well as a challenge in the knowledge that Einstein was fully human and flawed. Like the biblical saints, like the spiritual geniuses he admired—like all of us—Einstein made tragic mistakes and "muddled through" much of life.

I'm content, with Einstein as a guide, with "inklings" and "wonderings" about what I've come to grasp of the natural world from scientists and the places my conversation with them takes my theological imagination. Perhaps I am reaching, but let me reach. I'm not afraid, and the God I believe in honors knowledge and large, knowledgeable, seemingly unanswerable questions. Lyndon Eaves points out that even the great creeds of the church are working hypotheses—the best we've been able to come up with, but surely in a cosmic sense not the last word.

So—to leap—the Australian astrophysicist Paul Davies piques my imagination when we discuss Einstein's understanding of the relative nature of time. Davies is not a religious person in any traditional sense of the word, but he is openly intrigued by the spiritually evocative ideas he finds at the heart of the science he knows. Before Newton and Galileo, ancient cultures thought of time as organic, subjective, cyclical, and part of nature. Only in the nineteenth century did science and industry teach society to think of time as a matter of fixed precision. The railroads were being established, and it was important for people to be at the station on time. International and national time zones were necessary for doing business. Imagining time as an unstoppable arrow forward is a mind-set that our culture has largely inherited. Modern notions of progress hinge on this belief about time and so does the modern Western concept of selfhood, of personal identity accumulated through the passage of time. But Einstein discredited this. He described time as elastic, not absolute, curving and warping in response to matter and energy. Einstein referred to the human perception of time divided into past, present, and future as a "stubbornly persistent illusion." He restored time, Davies says provocatively, to its rightful place at the heart of nature.

Einstein also saw time as beginning with the origin of the universe. By inference, then, there must be such a thing as before time, or beyond time. Paul Davies goes so far as to say that this could be analogously imagined as the chaos or *om* or afterlife or dreamtime or nirvana that variously and luminously appear across the spectrum of the world's religious beliefs. He puts it this way:

> Einstein was the person to establish this notion of what is sometimes called block time—that the past, present, and future are just personal decompositions of time, and that the universe of past, present, and future

in some sense has an internal existence. And so even though individuals may come and go, their lives, which are in the past for their descendants, nevertheless still have some existence within this block time. Nothing takes that away. You may have your threescore years and ten measured by a date after your death. You are no more. And yet within this grander sweep of the timescape, nothing is changed. Your life is still there in its entirety.

And here is a memory this notion redeems for me, though it resolves nothing. My teacher Leander Keck's wife of many, many years was in the late stages of Alzheimer's disease when I landed on campus. He carried this fact and its concomitant grief softly, but publicly. I will never forget the day near the end of our year with the New Testament when he read to us from the wild, apocalyptic book of Revelation, as unpredictable a choice for the canon as any. From my upbringing I knew of the beast with the number 666 as a bizarre and merciless piece of imagery of end times and a vivid aspect of my grandfather's theology. I am not sure what to do with Revelation and am persuaded that the health of my soul in the here and now does not depend on it. But there is a famous line in the book of Revelation that I will forever hear in Leander Keck's voice, and that I will always imagine in bold as a point of the story:

> They shall hunger no more, neither thirst any
> more;
> The sun shall not strike them, nor any scorching
> heat.
> For the Lamb in the midst of the throne will be
> their shepherd,
> And he will guide them to springs of living water;
> And God will wipe away every tear from their eyes.

As he read this to us, tears filled his eyes. All of us knew he was thinking of his wife and the terrible grief of the last chapter of their life together. He was cleaving to that promise tucked between Revelation's demons and reckonings and battles: of a tender ultimate encounter with God when the sadness will be gathered up, the defects mended, the tears wiped away. We rose to our feet and applauded him and tears pricked our eyes as well and so did the promise in those lines. You could see this as selective reading, wishful thinking. But looking at the person of Leander Keck, I believed it with all my heart.

The physicist John Polkinghorne speaks of a pervasive human intuition of hope on a cosmic scale, life's bitterness and suffering notwithstanding—a sense that human beings cleave to even in the midst of darkness, illness, war, decay, and calamity. He treats this seriously as data, an accumulation of evidence too widespread to ignore. This is the same intuition that seems confirmed every time I hear Julian of Norwich's fourteenth-century mystical mantra: "All shall be well, and all shall be well, and all manner of thing shall be well." Julian threw herself at suffering—willing, praying fervently, to know the crucifixion of Christ from the inside—physical pain, mental torment, and all. She penned her "Showings" from mystical revelations she reported inside that answered prayer. She saw the world the size of a hazelnut in God's hand. She spoke of Christ "our mother." She also articulated a startling proposition that only good in the world is ultimately real—though evil has a power to inflict real suffering and pain within time. Julian herself was living through the Hundred Years' War and the Black Death as she wrote these lines—and that explains, I believe, why they land in our ears hundreds of years later with such integrity. Revelation wrapped in time and space, the mystic says along with the scientist, does not appear full-blown. If holiness is happening, it is happening in the thick of reality, not replacing the world we know, not banishing death, but defying its terror as the last word. And here is the task that fills my days: how to speak of this together and make it more visible, audible, and tangible in the world.

CHAPTER FOUR

SPEAKING OF FAITH

———

DEVELOP "EYES TO SEE AND EARS TO HEAR"—a biblical
injunction that has come to make great good sense to me.
Something mysterious happens when you train your eyes to
see differently, your ears to hear differently, to attend to what
you have been ignoring. The experienced world actually
changes shape. There are parallels to this idea, and versions
of "eyes to see and ears to hear" in every religious tradition
I've since come to know. It is a natural consequence of the
essential Buddhist drive to see reality, see human suffering
itself, so clearly, straight on, that you can see straight through

it. The ancient Celts, to whom I feel a kindred pull, speak of "thin places," even "thin times"—places and times where the veil between heaven and earth, between the temporal and the eternal, is worn thin. In snatches that come like gifts, our senses take in a different kind of reality. It sends us back with a lighter step and yet more passionately engaged into ordinary life.

I turned away from an active interest in public affairs in my years of religious discovery after Berlin. I internalized the words of Thomas Merton—an echo of a thousand voices that shaped me in that time—that the spiritual life "is the life of man's real self, the life of that interior self whose flame is often allowed to be smothered under the ashes of anxiety and futile concern." Newspapers magnified my anxiety and my awareness of problems too large and too far away for me to begin to imagine how to address. The power of story and image is profoundly operative in the realm of news, but here their force is blunt and one-dimensional. The pictures alone that make front pages often paralyze me with despair: bleeding bodies, starving children, scenes of devastation that moments before were the setting of ordinary, unsuspecting routine, irritation, and pleasure. And so I did not regularly read newspapers for years. They distracted, I felt, from the good it was in my grasp to affect and attain. I poured my energy into being present to those closest to me. I became a mother. I believed—and still believe—that when all is said and done, none of us will be measured on how much we accomplish but on how well we love. To honor the complexity of love that our culture denies is the true work of life, as Rilke describes in words that matched my new observations about life and the universe:

> People look for easy solutions, for the easiest way to the easy . . . but everything in nature grows and fights to grow and struggles at every cost and against all resistance to remain complete in itself and true to its fundamental nature . . . It is also good to love—love being difficult. Love is perhaps the most difficult task given us, the most extreme, the final proof and test, the work for which all other work is only preparation.

When I went "to work" in those early years of searching, it was to test my lofty, demanding new ideas about love and God and meaning in places of elemental individual struggle beyond the classroom. In New Haven I worked as a chaplain on the Alzheimer's and dementia floor—Wooster II—of a home and hospital for the elderly. The people there reversed all the rules of social discourse of the life I had led up to then. They would ask me my name but never remember it. They were not interested in my background and education, the places I'd seen, the titles I'd held—the credentials, in other words, with which I had presented and positioned myself in the world. They would only know whether I was kind, gentle, patient, a good listener. Unlike their children, spouses, and friends who were grieving the incremental loss of the person they had known for a lifetime, I had no memory of their former selves. I could come to know them and love them as they were now, and this was my greatest gift to them. But they gave me far more.

I have always been invested in ideas, in words, in the presentation of words. The people on Wooster II took me out of my head. They taught me the gravity of nonverbal presence—of eye contact and touch. I learned to accept silence, not to fill it with talk, to respect the immensity of what eyes and hands alone could express. The writings of Margaret Spufford came back to me on that dementia ward—the notion that in the end, the reality of God is most powerfully expressed not in ideas and proclamations but in presence. I sometimes felt that presence palpably in silence and the inchoate, searching bond of raw togetherness between us. I could not begin to take away their suffering. But I sat with it, with them. Sometimes we seemed to summon a palpable joy, a redemptive presence larger than ourselves, that made it all more bearable, if just in moments.

And for a summer Michael and I took on the salvation of a children's day camp in South Philadelphia: Camp Get-Along, a sweetly named effort to provide a haven for the wandering children of the city summer, and to reconcile the racial mistrust that infused city streets with an expectation of danger. The summer began with a series of menacing disasters, all of them caused by adults: broken promises, a budget that existed only on paper, a car accident. The multiracial, ecumenical steering committee that had hired us—inspiring on paper—was fraught with petty arguments and ego wars. The priest who hired us had neglected to find us a place to live, and so for a time we slept, ate, and planned on the dirty floor of our tiny office in the church. I learned to be wary that summer of a pious approach to life that saw good intentions and righteous prayer as substitutes for planning and pragmatic action. This way of faith only deepened the despair it was called to heal.

We came close to leaving many times in those early days. We were only stopped by the occasional visits of a stranger, a little boy. His name was Ted. Three times he banged on the door of that dilapidated church, on three of the worst days we had. He never smiled. He asked, "Is there going to be a camp here? Can I come?" His question forced us to recollect, each time, why we were there in the first place. His unsmiling face haunted us and kept us going. And in the end, a camp was made possible by remarkable single mothers and teenagers and other sundry, hardworking angels who joined their energy to ours. It was chaotic and gritty and repeatedly joyful and thoroughly miraculous.

The New Testament is full of mysterious accounts of Jesus appearing as a stranger after the resurrection to friends and followers, only to reveal himself when the practical love of hospitality is shared. As much as our culture puts the details of the crucifixion and resurrection under a microscope, I am surprised that neither scholars nor the Christian faithful ponder these Gospel stories—too numerous to ignore—of the risen Christ anonymously present in the world thereafter, a shape-shifter like the human confusion he accompanied and shed light on. In the Gospel of John, Jesus appears anonymously several times and finally to a few apostles, including Peter. Peter is the most hapless disciple of all, always getting things wrong. He has nevertheless been anointed by Jesus to become the "rock" of the church. On this occasion after the resurrection, Peter and the others suddenly recognize Jesus after they have offered this ostensible stranger something to eat. Three times at that meal Jesus asks Peter, "Do you love me?" Peter answers each time, "Yes,

Lord, you know that I love you." Jesus responds, in turn, "feed my lambs," "tend my sheep," "feed my sheep."

Three times Ted appeared to us that summer, asking if we could organize a difficult task so that he could have a place away from hot and hostile streets. I have a picture of him from that summer, which I always keep on my desk at work. He is swimming, and only his head is visible above the water. He is smiling the beautiful smile he unwrapped for us the second week of camp. His face is set off by what looks like Mediterranean blue, though it was only the public pool across the wide, dirty street. Ted's face remains the face of Christ for me: nine years old, black, delightful, heartbreaking, his smile a pure gift.

But I can't really care about Ted and other children like him, can I, and be content to blithely leave him there, frozen in time, nine years old and smiling, knowing that the world he's grown up into was stacked against him from the first? There were very clear limits to what I could do for Ted personally. I wouldn't come back to journalism and political curiosity for the same reasons I'd approached them earlier in my life, with eyes and ears convinced that these were the exclusively legitimate interpreters and arenas of meaningful action in the world. But I had to reckon with the hard longing for justice that is within me and that runs persistently alongside the work of practical care in Christianity and religious traditions as a whole. The Hebrew Bible's prophet Micah encapsulates this most wonderfully: "What does the Lord require of you, but to do justice, and to love kindness, and to walk humbly with your God?"

Years passed before I chose to notice that even the monk Merton didn't socially disengage and become politically mute. Merton, who took a vow of silence only to become a best-selling author in his twenties, became an increasingly political thinker in the decade of my birth—the decade, also, of his untimely death. In this he embodied the dual journey inward/journey outward that is followed by religious people and communities I admire the most. Merton's example as much as his words urged me in those early years of spiritual awakening not to give in to the anxiety the world described by the news left in me, but to beat it back with words and actions of my own. "Anxiety is the mark of spiritual insecurity," I had circled in black in my favorite of his books, *No Man Is an Island*:

> It is the fruit of unanswered questions. And there is a far worse anxiety, a far worse insecurity, which comes from being afraid to ask the right questions—because they might turn out to have no answer. One of the moral diseases we communicate to one an-

other in society comes from huddling together in the pale light of an insufficient
answer to a question we are afraid to ask.

Here in fact was Thomas Merton presaging how my own sense of purpose would evolve. I have given myself over to questions—large, hard, loving, full-blooded questions. I have become a crusader against insufficient questions and answers that stand in, prematurely and destructively, for both justice and mystery.

I began to find my way to do this at a Benedictine monastery, Saint John's Abbey, and its sister community, Saint Benedict's, down the road in central Minnesota—a part of the world I would once have imagined as the middle of nowhere. These Benedictines were, after my heart, contemplative and industrious at once. *Ora et Labore* is their motto—worship and work, simultaneous and inextricable. They live and teach, publish and pray on prairie their German forebears settled in 1856 in the midst of a devastating plague of grasshoppers. They take great pride in the fact that their order began in the sixth century, predating the major divisions of the church, and they draw ethical sustenance from a generous, sacred, not quite linear view of time. I emerged from divinity school with a sense of the vastness and relevance of the theological enterprise—the human search for words about God, and lives crafted in their resonance. But I could not find these aspects of religion visible in our public life. I could not find a way to trace their imprint until I fell down Collegeville's contemplative rabbit hole.

In the decade of my birth, the 1960s, while political America was protesting, loving not warring, warring not winning, dreaming spaceships and grieving, these monks were building. They lent creative genius to the liturgical renewal of the Roman Catholic Church before and after Vatican II, word of which had not reached my Southern Baptist childhood. They built a manuscript library that is becoming the world's greatest repository of formerly buried monastic treasures, now catalogued in microfiche and digital files for present and future generations. As it happens, Collegeville was also the birthplace in 1967 of my current employer, Minnesota Public Radio/American Public Media, which became a media phenomenon with a talent of comic brilliance, Garrison Keillor, and an entrepreneurial leader, a Saint John's alum named Bill Kling. But I first came under the spell of another, less media-savvy Saint John's progeny, a place of ecumenical conversation and research now called the Collegeville Institute. It remains small and quiet by choice, and has done mighty works in the world.

In 1995, I first spent a summer week at the institute. With fourteen soon-beloved strangers, I sat around a plain round conference table that I came to imagine as a rival, or at least a counterpart, to those self-important strategic conference tables of Berlin. Here, life and death, mystery and meaning, were all on the table. We engaged in a simple, life-changing exercise of reflecting on theological questions by looking back at our lives. That can sound reductive, and strictly personal. But time and space become more generous when we explore ultimate truths in the presence of others. "Thin places" open up. This experience is had in churches, synagogues, mosques, and temples all the time. It happens among friends and in marriages and at hospital bedsides. We make the discovery that when we are honest and vivid and particular in describing what is most personal and important in life, we can summon universal and redemptive places at the very edge of words. In Collegeville we did so in the act of engaging religious difference.

It's easy to forget these days that different kinds of Christians were at each other's throats in the name of piety for centuries. Islam is seven hundred years younger than Christianity, and roughly seven hundred years ago Christians were burning heretics at the stake, staging bloody inquisitions, and waging global holy wars. As late as the mid-1800s in the United States, there were outbreaks of Protestant mob violence against Catholics. Churches and entire neighborhoods burned. In this sermon from 1911, at the Cathedral of St. John the Divine—now a famously liberal congregation—the preacher mixed the virtue of separation of church and state, as was common then, with anti-Catholic rhetoric:

> We must fight to keep church and state forever separated. We must fight for our public schools, against the machinations of an Italian hierarchy that is today endeavoring to undermine and destroy them. Before it is too late and the hordes of Europe and Asia have engulfed us, let us arise and fight for Anglo-Saxon freedom and Anglo-Saxon discipline, for Almighty God who is still for us.

And through the first half of the twentieth century, most small American towns had virtual walls of religious segregation—not just Catholic churches and Protestant churches but Catholic pharmacies and Protestant pharmacies. Not to mention Catholic schools, because in earlier times in our great republic, Protestant legislators—that is to say, majority mainstream Americans—forbade Catholics from teaching in public schools, in the name of separation of church and state. Protestants were free citizens and democrats, the reasoning went, but Catholics would ineluctably be governed by the long hand of the Vatican. Meanwhile within Protestantism itself across the centuries, other divisions flourished—byzantine and deep. "Calvinist" and "Lutheran" and "Anglican" were not mere theological digressions but different ways of seeing the world. The splinters that came later—from Anabaptist to Mennonite to Holiness to Pentecostal—complicated matters further. Growing up in the 1950s, my mother was forbidden by her father to date the boy next door because he was Methodist. Thirty years and a far more tolerant world later, dear reader, she married him.

So religion has always been a volatile aspect of human life, even in the land of the free and the brave—because it has always been a container for more than itself. It has always become intertwined with that fraught human experience of identity. But progress is possible. As we agonize over interreligious hostility in the early twenty-first-century world, we might take note of the general rapprochement that has eventually taken hold between different kinds of Christians. Most Americans may not be card-carrying members of the National Council of Churches, but the idea of outright hostility between Protestants and Catholics as a cultural norm appears ludicrous. The battle lines that bloodlessly but bitterly divided families and communities are unimaginable. For the young, they are as incomprehensible as the Berlin Wall sounded to my daughter as we stood at the open Brandenburg Gate just a decade after the wall had fallen. Cars and bicycles drove past us between what had once been East and West and was now the free, vigorous heart of the city. I told her about the no-man's-land this had been in the Berlin I inhabited, about the watchtowers that had stood between the columns, the tank traps and barbed wire and attack dogs and guards with guns. She looked at me finally like I was delusional, and smiled forgivingly as she said, "Mom, I don't think they really had *guns*."

In Collegeville, I began to internalize the Benedictines' long, wise perspective on history—how bewildering and distracting its immediate lessons can be. They helped me grasp that when I say I sat around a table in Collegeville where Armenian Orthodox and Nazarene Holiness and Roman Catholic were gathered companionably together, that is really saying something.

And as the people around that table opened up one by one, taking their time and telling their stories, doctrine and tradition and religious history came alive before me. Our conversation of six days began with an intense, delightful Armenian Orthodox scholar who began his personal history six hundred years in the past, with the assassination of an ancestor who was a bishop. His fierce modern struggle for faith still found its source and counterweight in that drama.

One of our moderators was a Roman Catholic woman whose parents were Catholic intellectuals and writers. As the Second Vatican Council drew all the Catholic world to Rome for four years, she passed around canapés to her parents and their friends and inhaled the vast excitement and promise of that event. I imagine her as a girl hearing the dramatic statement of the council's convener, Pope John XXIII, that he intended "to shake off the dust that has collected on the throne of St. Peter since the time of Constantine, and let in some fresh air." She has devoted the rest of her life to dialogue between the Catholic Church and other traditions, dialogue that happens softly on the sidelines of world events but grows ever more critical in an interconnected world.

The funniest man around our table of often earnest, often intimate, discussion was a Nazarene Holiness church historian named Paul Bassett. He had been captured as a young scholar by the history of Iberian Christianity, the middle ages of Spain and Portugal, and so he became an expert on Christianity hundreds of years before his own tradition was born on the American frontier. People in his church ask him all the time, he says with amusement but not a hint of derision, when "real Christians" got to that part of the world. "I have to tell them," he says, "that those were real Christians there all along, and that's why the grace of forgiveness is so important." I had always thought of Holiness preachers as crazy snake handlers. But from Paul Bassett I first learned that the original Holiness pioneers were renegade Methodists who broke from churches they felt had grown materialistic, formalistic, and cold. They were abolitionists. The historic Seneca Falls meeting on women's suffrage was held in a Holiness church. The Salvation Army emerged from the Holiness Movement. This stranger of great warmth and dignity loved his church and I could see why. I felt that Paul Bassett might be a vision of the kind of Christian my grandfather could have been with a little more education—learned and passionately faithful and humble, with an endearing edge of wit.

In 1995, I was engaged to conduct an oral history of the institute. With its then-director, Patrick Henry, a man of immense energy and a large and generous intelligence, I drew up a list of fifty-five people whose lives and thought had intersected with the Collegeville Institute. This journey of conversation lasted for two years, and took me to both coasts as well as Atlanta, Chicago, and Rome. My conversation partners were lay and ordained, and some of them were among the great Christian thinkers of the twentieth century. They included the Yale historian Jaroslav Pelikan; the liberation theologian Robert McAfee Brown; the evangelical Christian philosopher Richard Mouw; the biblical scholar and later the first African American president of the National Council of Churches, Bishop Thomas Hoyt Jr.; and the prolific author and political activist Sr. Joan Chittister. They were all my teachers. And as different as they could be, there were recurring qualities in these people, constants that I came to associate with God and that I have continued to find in conversation with people across the world's traditions: thoughtfulness, humility, a sense of humor, and an openness to being surprised. Patrick Henry, who wrote a vibrant book called *An Ironic Christian's Companion*, always puts "a sense of irony" on his list of common qualities of great lived theology; I'll include that too.

In all of my nonreligious years in Europe, I had eschewed cathedrals and religious capitals. I had been to Florence and Venice but never to Rome. Now I spent five days there, in hours and hours of conversation with a Paulist priest, Tom Stransky. He had been Pope John XXIII's liaison to non-Catholic observers of Vatican II, and had later headed the Paulist order. Now he was running the Tantur Ecumenical Institute on the road between Jerusalem and Bethlehem, bringing Christians, Muslims, and Jews to speak together in the place in the world where their kinship was most obvious and also most prone to violence. Tom Stransky is an eccentric genius, and although I tend toward awe and affection at the good minds of others, I don't use that word lightly. He told me over one of our delicious dinners that week in Rome, after our interview for the day had finished, that he had published several works of poetry and fiction under a pseudonym. For all I know he has a double life as J. D. Salinger.

But in our formal interviews he also revealed to me the secrets of the Collegeville approach to conversation that had changed so many lives and was about to change mine. They call it the "first-person" approach—and that became the title of one of the early incarnations of my radio show. But that is too simple, and it didn't work as a show title. The first-person approach to religious speech is essentially about humanizing doctrine. It disallows abstractions about God, even as it takes account of the fact that it is hard, and so intimate, to speak about this aspect of life directly. The Quaker author Parker Palmer likens the nature of the soul to a wild animal deep in the woods of our psyche that if approached brusquely or cross-examined will simply run away. We have to create quiet, inviting, and trustworthy spaces, Parker says, to keep the insights and presence of soul at the table. And we put words around what the soul knows, Stransky told me, not through what we *think*, but through who we *are*, through the story of our lives.

There is a term, *narrative theology*, that also describes what the first-person approach elicits. St. Augustine's *Confessions*, Dietrich Bonhoeffer's *Letters and Papers from Prison*; Sr. Helen Prejean's *Dead Man Walking*—these are vivid and persuasive theological tracts, because they present religious ideas as forged and expressed in the language of life, of reality in the raw. Anne Lamott's salty religious memoirs are among the many lively contemporary examples. The Benedictines and their constellation of friends gave a new credence and context to my inborn, ingrained drive to be effective, pragmatic, real. But they changed my vision about that and taught me a whole new set of intellectual and creative tools to turn that vision into something useful for myself and others. From them I inherited the notion that everyone has relevant observations to make about the nature of God and ultimate things—that the raw material of our lives is stuff of which we construct our sensibility of meaning and purpose in this life, of how the divine intersects or interacts with our lives, of what it means to be human. I believe this with all of my heart, and I believe that we have too often diminished and narrowed the parameters of this quest. We've made it heady or emotional and neglected to take seriously the flawed, mundane physicality, the mess as well as the mystery, of the raw materials with which we are dealing.

And as I began to talk and travel for the oral history project, I conducted it in this spirit. I did not invite people of faith to pronounce. I asked them to trace the intersection of religious ideas with time and space and the color and complexity of real lives—not just the trajectory of their lives, but what they knew of the world, the work they did, who and what they loved. This both grounded and exalted what they had to say, and it let me in. I was most surprised at first by how listenable these conversations were, in dramatic contrast to the strident religious language of our public life. There is a profound difference between hearing someone say this is *the* truth, and hearing someone say this is *my* truth. You can disagree with another person's opinions; you can disagree with his doctrines; you can't disagree with his experience. What I heard invariably shed some light on an experience of mine, or lit up some corner of another faith that had been closed to me, mysterious and even forbidding. I could never again dismiss one of those traditions of my conversation partners wholesale, because it now carried the integrity of a particular life, a particular voice. People tell me that this is the effect of listening to the far-flung perspectives on *Speaking of Faith*, and this delights me.

My apartment-mate that first summer in Collegeville was the earthy theologian Roberta Bondi. I would interview her a year later at her home in Atlanta. When I met Roberta, she had just completed her wonderful theological autobiography, *Memories of God*. She taught me to approach my conversational theological premise—that we all come to understand God through the stories of our lives—in all its complexity. We confuse our heavenly father with our earthly father when we are children, Roberta notes, and this is a double-edged sword. Like me, she had grown up craving the love of an emotionally distant father and fearing the short-tempered God she had come to know in the tent revivals of her childhood. She became an atheist and an academic, a scholar of Semitic languages. One day, surrounded by ancient texts in the British Library, she began to read an obscure sixth-century text by a long-forgotten mystic, Philoxenus of Mabug, that spoke to her off the page. Through this dusty text, she told me, she encountered "a God who really was a God." She came to understand that God looks on us with a kindness and generosity and a sense of all the things we carry in our lives. This God, she told me, sees us with a great deal more allowance for our humanity than we ever make for each other or for ourselves. In all of my thinking and studying up to then, I had not dared to imagine a God with such softness toward me.

Following this discovery, Roberta took the desert fathers and mothers of the earliest church as her companions across time and space, her mentors in prayer. In the fourth, fifth, and sixth centuries, they started a minor cultural upheaval by retreating to empty spaces in search of God. Roman civilization was crumbling around them. They literally decamped to the deserts of Egypt and Syria and took up residence in caves and crags of mountain and the open air. The church, they felt, had been corrupted by its own success. Politicians and poets, military officers and mothers followed them for prayers, advice, and meaning.

I have come to think of the desert fathers and mothers as Christianity's first psychotherapists as well as mystics. They were early seekers of the Christian empire, out to demystify and recover the essence of religious teachings. In these lives of faith led in the light of ancient traditions, I again felt time acting more like a circle than a line. In the preface to Roberta's *Memories of God,* there is a paragraph that describes the frame of mind with which I embarked on this odyssey through the Christian landscape at the end of one century, and the method I would adapt for radio journalism across many religious traditions at the beginning of the next:

> At Collegeville, I finally accepted that the theological work of telling one another our stories, or talking about the ways in which our concrete and particular experiences intersected with the great Christian doctrines was not private work, or work done on behalf of each of us as individuals. It was a common work, real theology, done in order to find a way to claim for our own time and

our own generation what it means to be Christian.

Before I completed the journey Collegeville sent me on, I interviewed an extraordinary monk of St. John's, Godfrey Diekmann, a giant of liturgical reform before and after Vatican II. All the way through my project I had collected stories from luminaries and laypeople whose most vivid and beloved memories of Collegeville had to do with picking mushrooms with Godfrey. By the time I met Godfrey the year before his death, he was in his nineties and frail, no longer foraging for mushrooms nor openly changing the life of the church. But he was luminous. When I interviewed Studs Terkel at ninety-three he reminded me of Godfrey, though Studs calls himself an agnostic, which he defines with a smile as "a cowardly atheist." Like Godfrey he glowed with a life well lived, a life defined by words well chosen, by grand ideas elicited as well as offered, and by a web of life-giving relationships. Studs Terkel and Godfrey Diekmann look alike in my mind's eye: gray haired and flush faced, large and generous and full of light even as their bodies were traveling the end stretch of incarnation.

It was amazing to sit with Godfrey and hear his stories. They tumbled out of him, faster than my transcriber, later, could type. One of them, deeply moving, is of a gathering at

Yale of scholars working on the first cross-denominational Christian translation of the Bible. Someone suggested that they say a prayer to begin, but how to do that in a nonsectarian way? And who would lead? These were still awkward questions in the world just a few decades ago. A responsible committee, they turned to the Lord's Prayer, a petition straight from the Bible that Christians had been praying longer than the men in that room and their churches had been divided. And as Godfrey describes it, as they began to recite words in unison that they all knew by heart, their eyes filled with tears at the simplicity and the enormity of that act of common prayer. Godfrey remembered that moment as riveting, as they all realized for the first time—truly realized—that this text that preceded their divisions also transcended them in the most elemental way.

The longer he lives and loves and prays, Godfrey tells me with some urgency before I go, the more he believes that Christianity needs a renewed *incarnational* theology—a back-to-basics understanding of the implications of belief in a God who threw himself whole into the light and darkness of life with us. "All of creation in itself," he tells me, "has a certain dignity, a certain reality as the image of God's greatness and beauty and strength. But we have failed to see things. We have failed to hear things."

Godfrey's mushrooms, I understood after I finally met

him, were the perfect metaphor for his theology: a common slogging through beauty, getting rained on, getting dirty, taking in the fields' and forests' silent declaration of God, anticipating the delicious meal to come. This theology infused his understanding of doctrine, faith, and worship—not isolated ritual but an expression of the eternal in the concrete: muddy, of the earth, alive.

In 1998, I pitched the wild idea of a public radio program on religion to Bill Buzenberg at Minnesota Public Radio. Buzenberg had just come to Minnesota from running the news at National Public Radio. There he had started the religion desk because he had seen spirituality and religion rising as an interest in popular culture and in listeners' lives. I pointed him to polls that consistently showed a broad majority of Americans believed in God, considered religion important in their lives, prayed. Over 80 percent continued to be nominally Christian, interesting enough in itself, while other spiritual allegiances were animating pluralism in our culture. This was not always the traditionally rooted, institution-based religion of our parents and grandparents, but it was searching, lively, and literate. In those days when I was making the case for a program dedicated to religious voices and ideas, I would also point to trends in publishing—the fact that by the late nineties, books with religious and spiritual titles had been growing explosively for a decade, bucking the trend in virtually every other subject matter. Sr. Joan Chittister calls this "getting church off the shelves." If religious institutions can't or won't answer the burning questions of our time, Chittister says, human beings will seek elsewhere, and in the end this might contribute to the revitalization of traditions. In national political discourse by the late nineties, Falwell and Robertson weren't dominating the news as they once had, but religious passions were beginning to show themselves more consistently, and stubbornly, in the thick of our public life. *Newsweek* and *Time* had long ago stopped wondering about the death of God.

Still, many were skeptical that this subject belonged on public radio airwaves that stand for intelligence, relevance, and balance. Interestingly, those are words our listeners often use to describe the program they now hear. But I understood the fears and the enduring skepticism, then and now. We have had few models in our public life for religious speech that does not proselytize, exclude, anger, or offend. Traditional journalistic approaches did not convey the intellectual and spiritual content of religious perspectives. And the voices that threw themselves before microphones, using religious words and given credence as religious opinion leaders, betrayed that content flagrantly. But most basically, I think, intellectual blinders about religion in parts of our culture didn't drop easily, and they hang on in some quarters even now. Journalists and intellectuals and analysts who emerged from twentieth-century halls of learning and political culture were not trained to take religion seriously, to see and hear its humanity, its force in culture, its power to mobilize lives and communities. They were taught to maintain a professional ethos of distance and dismissal—even if religion retained a power in their private, personal lives. The mobilization of evangelical Christians in the 2000 election was treated by many of these thinkers and journalists as a fluke, if an electorally decisive and jarring one.

September 11, 2001, gave my fledgling radio project a new beginning—an infusion of raw terror and news relevance that made everything easier, and that I would never have wished for. Most obviously, Islam was on America's map of the world and on mine in a new way. Islam is the lived faith and container of identity for over 1.2 billion human beings. Given that scale, this tradition did not figure proportionately in the imagination and education of Americans before 9/11. Of course Islam had been among us—six million Muslims in the United States alone and that number growing rapidly, one third of them African American. And this is for the most part a quiet, gentle lived faith. But in mainstream American society it was indisputably "other." Our public dialogue was immediately full of pundits either foretelling a clash of civilizations or voicing platitudes about Islam as a religion of peace. I was never convinced that either reaction provided us a substantive way forward, as neither history nor religion ever play themselves out in black and white. Islam is an astonishingly plural, inclusive faith in the broad sweep of its history and its theology. That history and that theology were stolen from view by unforgettable images of airplanes crashing into buildings. They continue to be eclipsed by other escalating forms of violence.

In the days and months after 9/11, Americans wanted to hear Muslims condemning the terrorists with a recognizable vocabulary—decrying them as evil, forsaking religion itself if it could inspire such an act. To some extent, we haven't listened as Muslims have expressed their grief and outrage, and to some extent they have done so most poignantly in private, internal dialogues. In my work I set out to hear Muslims speak from the depths of their faith. This has been a great surprise for me, and a source of tremendous learning, sadness, and hope. In important ways, my encounter with Islam has been a new kind of reminder of the limits of words—of merely *speaking* of faith. Muslims' very way of approaching religious convictions and questions is different from the Christian and Judaic modes of discourse U.S culture long ago internalized as normal, and it is therefore easily obscured in American ears. Our culture tends to define a religion in terms of what its adherents "believe"; this is a very Protestant Christian approach. But Islam is not primarily a religion of beliefs but of practices, of piety woven into the fabric of daily individual and communal life.

Islamic piety also takes literary, musical, and aesthetic forms as seriously as word and argument—more seriously perhaps. My Muslim conversation partners have taught me so much about Islam that is beautiful and intriguing, gentle and quiet. And so much of it falls within the realm of religious intimacy. It is not readily accessible to outsiders. I will never forget my early interviews with a young Iranian American Islamic scholar, Omid Safi, and Seemi Ghazi, a Pakistani American educator and lay reciter of the Qur'an. Qur'anic Arabic emerged as a new language within a language in the seventh century in Arabia and then Persia and enriched already robustly poetic linguistic worlds. The Prophet Muhammad surrounded himself with poets, and was often greeted with poetry in his travels. Omid Safi walked me through love poetry that today forms the spirituality of illiterate Iranian shepherds; music that evokes the heart of Islam for ordinary people in places like Afghanistan, Turkey, and Pakistan; the gorgeous vocabulary and verse that grounds the Islamic mystical tradition, Sufism. Seemi Ghazi described learning Qur'an by hearing its cadences long before she could understand its words, as many Muslim children do, learning it as one with the rhythm of her mother's voice and breath and heartbeat.

Here is the most important point Muslims have pressed home to me: the Qur'an is not meant to be read as words on a page and merely intellectually appropriated. The Qur'an is aurally and inwardly digested. The word *Qur'an* means "recitation," but even that word is inadequate. The Qur'an's intrinsic beauty forms an essential part of its mystery and its message. Wielding isolated Bible verses to make a point—"proof-texting"—is an irritating but well-worn practice in the part of the Christian world in which I grew up. It is a new phenomenon in Islam. After 9/11, non-Muslims couldn't know the strangeness and violence in the act of ripping and pronouncing verses of the Qur'an out of context.

I don't examine the great virtues of Islam in order to excuse cancers that have grown at its heart in our time, such as terrorist and sectarian violence and a virulent anti-Semitism. But in order to imagine a future in which those malignancies are not definitive, we must see Islam in the sweep of its history and theology. At its core Islam is a remarkably egalitarian faith, and this helps explain the profound and complex roots it has been able to sink in multitudinous cultures. I believe it also helps explain the vibrant and peaceable integration of a growing Muslim faith in U.S. culture, a phenomenon that has gone largely unremarked alongside news coverage of

Islamic unrest in other parts of the world. In 2006, the Islamic Society of North America elected a woman as its president—a Canadian convert to Islam, a supremely articulate and confident scholar, Ingrid Mattson. Omid Safi has become a leading voice in an energetic convergence of idea and action that calls itself "progressive Islam." And new generations of educated and empowered Islamic women—some of them daughters of previous generations of secular Islamic elites—are fashioning a way of life that incorporates religious tradition with a commitment to realizing the egalitarian impulse at the heart of Islam. They draw sustenance from Islamic traditions and women going back to the lifetime of the Prophet. Many choose to wear traditional Islamic dress and headdress, the *hijab*. And this complicates Western culture's ability to see them as free and strong.

As the Egyptian American scholar Leila Ahmed helped me see, Westerners have long had an impossible time seeing beyond the *hijab* to the human being behind it. A nineteenth-century British missionary described Muslim women "buried alive beneath the veil," and this way of seeing has largely carried over to Western imaginations about Islamic women into the present. Women like Leila Ahmed do not deny the violence and oppression of women that does characterize life in many Islamic cultures, especially in parts of the world where men and women are impoverished and uneducated.

She has written a groundbreaking study, *Women and Gender in Islam: Historical Roots of a Modern Debate*. But she says this:

> When people think about Muslim women, they think of the image of Saudi Arabia or Afghanistan. Why is that, when 90 percent of the Muslim world does not wear any of this stuff? And why is it that I never get called by a journalist—I get constantly called and asked to explain why Islam oppresses women—I have never yet been asked, "Why is it that Islam has produced seven women prime ministers or heads of state and Europe only two or three?"

Exclusionary Islamic violence is a reality of the twenty-first century. But it is not the whole story.

The religious historian Karen Armstrong has been struck in her own scholarship by the fact that all of the great religious traditions arose in times of extreme violence. They arose, to a one, to address that violence—to name and temper the egotism, fear, greed, and hatred behind it. And yet, paradoxically and organically, this violence became woven into the religions themselves. Violence in the surrounding world seeped into sacred scriptures. On one page of the Bible, for example, Armstrong points out that God is telling the people of Israel not to kill, and then a few pages later God tells them to wipe out all the inhabitants of Canaan. Jesus, in the New Testament, tells his followers to turn the other cheek, but in the Book of Revelation, Jesus is leading armies and destroying the enemies of God in battle with great gusto.

This dynamic plays itself out more overtly in the pages of the Qur'an. One profound difference between the origins of Christianity and of Islam—a dynamic that finds tragic expression in the hands of extremists—is that the Prophet Muhammad, unlike Jesus, was a political and military leader. His religious innovation unfolded with social and political consequences in the course of his lifetime. He waged real-time wars and negotiated real-world peace. There are spiritual sections of the Qur'an that young Muslims learn early and formatively; but there are also narratives of battle with the Prophet in the lead. Karen Armstrong puts this into perspective, and relates its redemptive lessons for the present, in this way:

> There are moments when Muhammad is
> the general saying, "You've got to fight hard.
> You've got to fight the enemy wherever you
> find them," as any general has to do. But

then he teaches, ultimately, that forgiveness is better. Ultimately, if the enemy seeks peace, you've got to lay down your arms immediately. And when we look around the world at many of these conflicts, it's not that religion has sparked these traditions, it's rather that violence has become endemic in a region and religion has got sucked into that vortex of violence. The Arab-Israeli conflict began on both sides as a secular conflict. Zionism was originally a secular movement, a secular revolution against religious Judaism, and the PLO was essentially secular liberation ideology.

The lesson is, let's settle disputes while we can, while they're still secular—and therefore capable of a pragmatic solution—before they fester, become sacralized and therefore the issues have become absolute. Because we can use a God horribly simply to endorse our own fears and loathings and hatred, and then you get horrors like September the eleventh. You get the atrocities of centuries ago of the Crusades, because people are not disciplined enough in realizing that God is not just a bigger and better version of ourselves writ large, with our likes and dislikes, but a reality that is entirely different.

We know more about the Prophet Muhammad than about Jesus or Moses or the founder of almost any other major tradition, because he came later in history. There's more documentation. And his first biographers set out to write history and present the Prophet, "warts and all," Armstrong says. They didn't attempt to whitewash him. They showed him having trouble with his wives. "People often assume that Muhammad had a wonderful harem and was basking decadently in a garden of sensual delights," she says. "Far from it. I mean, the wives were often a headache and undertaken for political reasons." But for Karen Armstrong—former nun, amateur theologian, religious intellectual, and now a self-proclaimed "freelance monotheist"—the three-dimensional knowledge we possess about Islam's founder can ultimately be a source of practical strength for Muslims and others. This idea has been echoed by my Muslim conversation partners these last years. They describe the Prophet as the humane, human model of virtue that can serve as a model for inner Islamic reform. Armstrong says,

You see him struggling. He was living in a violent and desperate, brutal society, and he managed to bring peace to that world. For five or six years he and the Muslims were fighting a war against Mecca. Because the Meccans were going to exterminate the little Muslim community, Muslims were fighting for their lives. But he won not by violence, but by eschewing violence, and for two years practicing a campaign of nonviolence that's not dissimilar to that practiced by Gandhi or other inspiring peaceable rulers. And you see his vulnerability. You don't often see Jesus laughing in the Gospels. In fact, I think you almost never do. You often see Muhammad playing with his grandchildren, putting little Hassan and Hussein on his shoulders and running around with them, weeping over a death of a friend, comforting his daughters, striving and sweating literally with the effort as he uttered the words—beautiful words of the Qur'an. The Qur'an doesn't come out well in translation, but the Arabic is just of surpassing beauty.

Muhammad was one of the great prophets, but also a poet and a statesman. In recent years, of course, with the horrors that have been perpetrated in the name of the tradition that he founded, he would have been so shocked, appalled, and devastated to see what has been done.

My Muslim conversation partners these past years have been Asian, African, Arab, and North American. They are appalled and devastated. They have also helped me see how and why Muslims across the world have limited resilience to bring to this moment of crisis. Blanket hatred of "the other"—such as the anti-Semitism that flourishes in many Muslim cultures today—is always an abstracted projection of personal and collective anxieties and fears. I know this also from my familiarity with Germany's anti-Semitic hysteria and genocide. My Muslim conversation partners have introduced me to contemporary Muslim people and cultures on edge—from fault lines that have been building since the rise of Wahhabism in the eighteenth century, to lingering wounds from colonialism in virtually every majority Muslim culture. In these places, the post–Cold War panaceas of progress—democracy and market economies and personal freedom—have faltered and fallen short. Globalization has put such failures and discrepancies on ubiquitous, garish display. Muslims' sense of being on the losing side of modernity has intensified with the ongoing war and chaos in Iraq, cultural clashes in western Europe, and scandals like Abu Ghraib. In contrast to the magnificence of what should be possible, despair becomes intolerable. This is not the enforced absence of hope, as I saw in East Germany. It is the mobilizing experience of hope betrayed.

I've been helped by the Islamic scholar Vincent Cornell's analysis that violent Islamists practice and propagate a "radically superficial" version of that faith. They've innovated and propagated a version of Islam that can be reduced to pronouncements and ideologies. Like fundamentalists of many stripes, they've effectively turned the tools of modernity against itself. Al Qaeda has used globalization's means of communication, travel, and technology to disseminate a radical "corporate brand" of Islam. This is a crisis of the first order within Islam, not first a battle of Islam with the West. Islamic extremists have killed many more Muslims than non-Muslims and continue to do so. Cornell and others depict the present as a time of ferment in Islam not so unlike the violent turmoil that preceded and accompanied the Christian Reformation. But the Spanish Inquisition was not televised, nor were its atrocities available for viewing on the Internet. The "terrorizers" of the Thirty Years' War did not have modern travel, communications, and weaponry at their disposal. And so in a very basic sense, the questions and dilemmas facing Islam address all of us. They are our questions, our dilemmas.

The Islamic scholar Seyyed Hossein Nasr says that U.S. policymakers and citizens are inclined, as he puts it, to "absolutize the transient" as we analyze Islam's problems and form responses. For example, we don't approach the creation of democracy in predominantly Muslim societies in our age as it in fact developed centuries ago at the birth of our own predominantly Protestant Christian republic—seething with religious energies and motivations and voices. Instead, we promote the secularized Western idea of society that evolved only in the last half century. And insisting that there can be no excuse for terror, we reject self-critical inquiry into the motivating political and psychological despair of young Muslim suicide bombers. We forget that at various stages in our own history—e.g., the civil rights movement—we have managed to simultaneously punish crime while also tending to the despair at its core as a matter of survival. We did not do so in order to excuse violence, but to prevent its repetition in future generations.

It is almost a cliché these days to note that Al Qaeda appeals to youthful despair, manipulates and makes it deadly. But I think we pause too rarely simply to mourn this human tragedy, to ask how we can mobilize against it. Shortly after

9/11, I spoke with three former fundamentalists—Christian, Jewish, and Muslim—in order to try to understand the suicide-bomber mentality. I was struck by their common emphasis on the exuberance of youth and the corresponding, if delusionary, exhilaration of religious radicalism. It was intoxicating, "a high," a thrill that met the adolescent hunger for thrills and also validation and empowerment. Khaled Abou El Fadl is a professor of law at UCLA and a global human rights activist. His story contains in itself the toxic brew of youth, human nature, economic deprivation, ethnicity, and global politics that so endanger our world today. He's spoken out against Islamic extremism—he prefers the words *supremacist* and *puritan* to *fundamentalist*—under threat of death. But growing up as a teenager in Egypt, he describes a narrow escape from that path.

As an Egyptian, everywhere you turn the identity to which you belong is confronted with military defeats. If you travel, you carry an Egyptian passport and you become thrown into a category of the inferior just by virtue of the fact that you belong to an Arab identity. And I remember, you know, going through a stage where I tried the sort of cool route of being Westernized. That, for me, didn't work, and what did work was that ex-ultation, intoxication, remarkable high of finding a group of people that tell you, "You know what? You're better than the Ameri-cans. You're better than the British. You're better than the Arabs. You're better than the Turks. You're better than anyone because you're Muslim and all you have to do is just simply accept our version of orthodoxy."

And I remember, as a teenager, suddenly I would walk around with my head high. I belonged to something very powerful. And I could see the world as black and white, evil and good. And I was not just on the side of good—anyone who wants to achieve good-ness has to come through me. You know, they have to get my approval. Fortunately, I grew out of it. Unfortunately, many of these kids never get that chance.

A young Muslim American activist, Eboo Patel, drives this point home more provocatively. He has just entered his thirties. He is ambitious, and his own energy is vast. He thinks about the phenomenon of young people involved in religious violence primarily through thinking about what young people want. He quotes a line by the poet Gwendolyn Brooks, "Boy Breaks Glass": "I shall create if not a note, a hole. If not an overture, a desecration." Patel adds,

> Young people want to impact the world. They want their footprint on Earth, and they're going to do it somehow. And if the only way that they get a chance to do that is by destroying things, then we shouldn't be surprised if that's the path they take. So when people say to me, "Oh, Eboo, you know, you run this sweet little organization called the Interfaith Youth Core, and you do such nice things, you bring kids together," I say, "Yeah, you know, there's another youth organization out there. It's called Al Qaeda, and Al Qaeda's been built over the past twenty-five years with lots of money and with lots of strategy and with lots of ideas of how you recruit young people and get them to think that this is the best way they can impact the world."

Eboo Patel also reminds me, when we speak, that heroic religious and social icons of the past century—such as Martin Luther King Jr. and Mahatma Gandhi—were in their twenties when they began to change the world. Moreover, as they transformed cultures less pluralistic than our own, these extraordinary reformers knew each other and worked together across traditions. Eboo Patel draws sustenance from interreligious images many of us have forgotten: Rabbi Abraham Joshua Heschel marching with Martin Luther King Jr. in Selma, saying that he felt as though his legs were praying; the Baptist minister King consulting with the Hindu Gandhi; and Gandhi sitting alongside the Pashtun Abdul Ghaffar Khan in Indian villages where Hindu-Muslim tensions threatened, reciting alternately from the Qur'an and the Bhagavad Gita, insisting that "the word of God" be heard.

Yet of all the differences between Eboo Patel and his Catholic, Mormon, Hindu, and Jewish friends growing up in suburban Chicago, he says, personal religious beliefs were the most difficult to talk about. He believes there is a salutary and practical power in giving young people fluency in the depths of their own religious traditions and those of others. He does so by first engaging adolescents and young adults in ground-level interactions based on service to others. He calls this work "track-two diplomacy." In many cultures, he has found, religious elders and leaders can be reluctant to engage openly with differing beliefs. But their children are open to meaningful interaction and the possibility of change.

More compellingly than words in Islam's defense, my Muslim conversation partners these past years have *evoked* gentleness and generosity, humility and civilization, and the possibility of peace. Most critically and counterintuitively, perhaps, they have reminded me and my listeners over and over that "they" are also "us."

From the late 1980s to the mid-1990s, before fundamentalism had become a household word, the religious historian Martin Marty directed a groundbreaking study of fundamentalisms in twenty-three religions around the world. Fundamentalism is never "old-time religion," he says. It is a modern phenomenon—by which he as a historian means roughly the last two hundred years. It is always reactive, born when there is an assault on values that people have *and are uncertain about.* And around the world in our time, he says, people are having trouble with identity—what do I believe, whom do I trust, who trusts me? The Fundamentalism Project crafted an evocative conclusion—that there is presently a "massive, convulsive ingathering of peoples into their separatenesses and overagainstnesses to protect their pride and power and place from others who are doing the same thing." In the United States this doesn't manifest itself usually in violent insurgencies or terrorism. It does appear in a cultural readiness to divide the world up into us and them, virtuous and vicious, good and evil.

I find a great deal of paradox in the insight Marty and others give me of fundamentalist religion, and paradox always gives me hope. It means there are tensions that long for resolution, gaps that might be pried open by human understanding and connection. For example, fundamentalists treat sacred text literally and at the same time highly selectively. Christian fundamentalists play fast and loose with the apocalyptic imagery in the Bible—seeing it as a kind of coded revelation—and they make leaps of fantasy to decode it. Thus many traditional conservative Protestants, like my grandfather, earnestly saw the pope as the antichrist in disguise. But it is hard to sustain such an interpretation as conservative Catholics join with fundamentalist Christians and others on some of the flagship moral values issues of our day. Even in the midst of what might look to some like reactionary religious alliances, exclusionary theology is being revised.

Christian fundamentalism took the original evangelical break from traditional Protestantism a step further. That is, in a world grown complex, threatening, and incomprehensible, fundamentalists retreated altogether from social issues and focused their energies on concern for what Marty calls "the zones closest to the self"—issues of worldview, identity, sexuality, gender differentiation, family, education, and communication. What's so interesting today, he remarks, is that as these groups have become part of a more politically activist conservative bloc, the public issues they champion are not social issues, they're "personal enlarged." And Marty floats a hypothesis that the debates will shift on these issues as they touch the personal lives of those engaged in fearing and resisting them. Laws on gay rights and practices, he believes, "will be changed when every tenth evangelical minister's daughter comes out. When it's close to you, you see it differently."

There is also a deep paradox in fundamentalism's adroit use of technology. Radio, television, and the Internet have been primary drivers of these movements that arise, in part, to protest technological advances that are destroying family, community, and morality. Marty tells this story:

I once spoke in a conservative church and the pulpit looked like a 747 panel. Red light would go on, a baby's crying in nursery 23C, and another blue light, and that means a

Jaguar's lights were left on in parking lot D. I could raise the temperature or the volume and everything else. And the minister in his sermon later blasted technology—which he was using. Well I can go into a liberal Methodist church and I'm pretty sure the microphone won't work . . . I'm kidding . . . But the Ayatollah Khomeini's revolution was done through tape recordings from France. Al Qaeda is very much at home with the Internet.

In the end, Martin Marty doesn't divide the world into conservative and liberal. He divides it into "mean and non-mean." Billy Graham, who ushered in a gentler, earlier tradition of evangelical religious influence in politics, was not mean. Some of his descendants are, and so are some liberals. As the specter of the fundamentalist religious identity of Al Qaeda has come to overshadow international affairs and identities, Marty has this advice for policymakers and citizens that echoes everything I learn in my life of conversation: Don't lump the faithful and fundamentalists together in any tradition. Don't demonize any group of religious people as an enemy. There is great diversity whenever large numbers of human beings are involved. Do all that you can to help them show their varieties and make it easier for them to be diverse. Make it easier for moderates in all of these movements to be moderates. Marty helps me better understand an important side effect of the work I do. *Speaking of Faith* is among a growing number of spaces in our culture for intelligent, innovative, and moderate religious voices to in fact serve as *moderators* within their traditions and our culture—to be seen and heard and to act. Marty himself only speaks of religious movements in the plural—as Protestantisms and evangelicalisms and fundamentalisms. In the simple act of pluralizing these broad categories of faith, he defies their use as ideological boxes, wedges, and bludgeons.

The reasoned and moderate Muslim center will not be secular, nor will the Christian or Hindu or Mormon or Jewish center. Developing eyes and ears for moderation does not mean denying the importance of religion in human life. It means inviting and enabling the devout to bring the best of their tradition to bear in the world. In the macroeconomic, macropolitical, macroreligious sphere, as much as in our private lives, we must develop eyes to see and ears to hear. Islam offers nothing more and nothing less than the gentle lived faith of ordinary Muslims—at home and at school, in hospitals and in soup kitchens—to counter indelible images of airplanes crashing into buildings. To train our eyes on that is to accept the challenging idea that I live by, that my guests live by: that each person's presence, action, and words in the world matter, however inconsequential they may seem against the backdrop of this evening's news. Religions remind us of this fact, this faith. Like any political or economic theory, this is empirically unverifiable. I choose it. Week after week, my conversation partners illuminate the imaginative and pragmatic possibilities of this choice.

The precarious collusion of political and spiritual frailty is quintessentially, tragically embodied in the intractable conflict in the common Holy Land of Christians, Muslims, and Jews. This is a root crisis of the contemporary world. It is a root crisis of Islam's internal ferment. At the best of times, the American Israeli journalist Yossi Klein Halevi once said to me, life in the Holy Land feels like a crossroads with apocalypse on the one side and collective transcendence on the other.

I first interviewed Yossi Klein Halevi in early 2002. He grew up in Brooklyn, the son of a Holocaust survivor, and became a Jewish extremist in his youth—elated, very much like Khaled Abou El Fadl, by the unparalleled sense of power and entitlement this bestowed. But he extricated himself, moved to Israel, and became a journalist. And in the bright days of the Oslo peace process of the 1990s, he made an exhilarating journey to know and pray with Palestinians. He wrote a beautiful, hopeful book, *At the Entrance to the Gar-*

den of Eden: A Jew's Search for Hope with Christians and Muslims in the Holy Land. I still believe that this is one of the most important spiritual memoirs of our time. But the Oslo process that made his journey possible was undermined by extremists on both sides from the first. It ended, finally, after the secular general Ariel Sharon made a controversial visit to a Muslim holy site, the Al Aqsa Mosque. By the time I spoke with Halevi, suicide bombings were targeting buses and cafés in Israeli cities. Halevi's spiritual homeland of Jerusalem had come to feel like a war zone. I have wished all these years that something would happen to make his despair in that program obsolete. But it remains tragically, repeatedly, current.

It is nearly impossible for an American to imagine the time warp that Israelis and Palestinians coinhabit. Political and spiritual energies are enmeshed and also held within other, larger histories—the biblical drama of ancient Israel and the tragedy of the twentieth-century Holocaust; the politics of the British Empire, the Ottoman Empire, and the Cold War; the histories of Christianity and Islam and of the disparate, intertwining cultures we now call the Middle East. The Oslo process accomplished a remarkable feat in raising both Palestinian and Israeli spirits. Hope in the Holy Land is as animating and volatile as anywhere on earth. The dashing of that hope accounts, in part, for the bitterness of recent times.

I interviewed Halevi again for a series of programs in 2006. I interviewed two Palestinians at the same time, Mohammad Abu Nimer at American University and Sami Adwan on the West Bank. I spent hours studying maps and pictures, reading timelines with subtle variations in emphasis that make the difference, in contrasting Palestinian and Israeli readings, between fact and interpretation. I quickly found myself entangled in the knot that Palestinians and Israelis describe alike, of two distinct narratives for the same lived history. One man's "independence" is another man's "catastrophe." One man's "hero" is another man's "terrorist." One man's "emigrant" is another man's "refugee." These are not merely contrasts of vocabulary but of experience, imagination, and possibility. They stand between these two peoples and any kind of sustainable peace.

As I sought to trace the contours of the relationship between religion and politics in the Holy Land, I was forced to finally and utterly discard my dismissive impatience with political processes. They can be necessary even for spiritual progress. Israelis and Palestinians who are not consumed by an understandable bitterness model a clarity that I seek to learn from. They know that mutually acceptable borders and balances of power are requisite foundation stones for collective human, spiritual reconciliation in their land. Prayer may also be essential, but it is not enough.

At the same time, they helped me see anew why we in the West need to learn to bracket religion *in* rather than *out* of our view of the world. My Palestinian and Israeli conversation partners these past years, good people all, don't agree on much. But they have told me with one voice that the Oslo peace process failed in part because it attempted to bracket out religious instincts on all sides of the conflict. This only succeeded in marginalizing moderate religious voices. Religious extremists insert themselves into the process in the Holy Land and elsewhere whether they are invited or not. To regret and ignore the volatile role of religion in the contemporary world will get us nowhere. It cripples our effectiveness, in Afghanistan and Iran as in the Holy Land and Iraq.

In the early days of the U.S. military presence in Iraq, I spoke with Ahmed al-Rahim, a young Iraqi American Harvard scholar. He had consulted with the early Coalition authority in Iraq of General Jay Garner, exploring how the United States might be an effective presence in revitalizing the educational system of that country. Such concerns sound remote and idealistic in the face of the everyday brutality that now consumes U.S. and Iraqi attention and planning. Al-Rahim is Muslim by upbringing, yet personally more secular than devout. Still, he worried with me, in those early, more hopeful days, that American preconceptions about the separation of religion from democracy were precluding a robust vision for the development of Iraqi civil society. Why, he asked, weren't Americans on the ground in Iraq fostering the development of Muslim chambers of commerce in local communities, empowering the grassroots goodwill and participation of secular-to-moderate Muslim businesspeople? Weren't the Christian-based Rotary Clubs and YMCAs building blocks of modern American civil society and democracy—building blocks that have secularized organically, peaceably, with the passage of time? Our clumsy grasp of the role of religion in different societies, like doomsday predictions of the danger of the theocracy in our own, are based on selective tellings of our own history.

Here is what de Tocqueville saw when he analyzed the young—fifty-five-year-old—American democracy in 1831:

> Religion in America takes no direct part in
> the government of society, but it must be re-
> garded as the first of their political institu-

tions. I do not know whether all Americans have a sincere faith and religion, for who can search the human heart? But I am certain that they hold it to be indispensable to the maintenance of republican institutions. This opinion is not peculiar to a class of citizens or to a party, but it belongs to the whole nation and to every rank of society.

People often ask me if I think the virtue of separation of church and state is endangered in our time. What I think, after looking at history with new eyes and ears, is that this brilliant virtue of the U.S. system has always been a work in progress. The words *separation of church and state* appear nowhere in the Constitution. The First Amendment called specifically for an end to established churches and for a concomitant preservation of religious liberty in the life of the republic as a whole. Thomas Jefferson first interpreted this to imply "a wall of separation" in a letter to a congregation of Baptists in Danbury, Connecticut, on January 1, 1802. But those Danbury Baptists rejected Jefferson's reading of the First Amendment, and the phrase was not enshrined in constitutional law until 1947. Until the twentieth century, there was no formal "atheist" voice with influence in American culture. The meaning of separation of church and state was debated and developed with different kinds of religious voices on every side of every argument.

Martin Marty likes to quote another founding father, James Madison, when he observes that we have never in fact had a *wall* of separation but a *line*. The line has shifted many times, sometimes subtly and sometimes dramatically. I am not deeply concerned by the fact that in our time the line once again is being tested. It simply gives me a renewed sense of the possibility and responsibility of the present. The University of Chicago legal historian Philip Hamberger suggests provocatively, after his own study of the evolving meaning of separation of church and state in U.S. history, that a too-brittle twentieth-century definition allowed U.S. culture to avoid grappling head-on with rising religious pluralism within our own culture. This was a counterpart to not seeing the complexity and implications of religion in other parts of the world. A certain compartmentalization of private reverence from public activity came naturally to many Christian and Jewish Americans, but this arguably divided us from the inside. The wall formed inside each of us, and this was not sustainable with human nature. I suspect that the multiplicity of religious energies in the twenty-first century may reshape, and enrich, the virtue of separation of church and state far more profoundly than the cyclical electoral successes of evangelical Christians or whichever parties succeed them.

In his book, *The Buddha in the World,* the Indian journalist Pankaj Mishra presents a fascinating take on global realities based on the social philosophy of the Buddha. Mishra went in search of the historical Buddha, a man of a particular time and place. Buddha neither claimed to be divine nor, as Pankaj Mishra stresses, did he mean to create a religion. But his human identity became ethereal and abstracted. The story of the beginnings of his life and his calling—his upbringing as a prince in a palace, his dramatic change of life after he encountered human misery for the first time—was passed down as an outline that rings of fairy tale. For many centuries Buddhism was lost in India, the country of the Buddha's birth, and left to be "discovered" by nineteenth-century Western colonizers, archaeologists, and explorers. Pankaj Mishra grew up in late-twentieth-century India imagining Buddha as one of the many Hindu gods his parents worshipped.

Mishra was an intellectual, in any case, with little interest in India's spiritual past. Then, to his surprise, he found the ideas and legacy of the Buddha turning up in the writings of great Western thinkers like Rilke and Hermann

Hesse, Schopenhauer and Einstein. The skeptic's skeptic, Friedrich Nietzsche, claimed the Buddha as a kindred spirit—a philosopher who could speak to his own age of breathtaking change and social, political, and religious upheaval. In the Buddha's historical origins in India, Mishra found a world that echoed the confusion and violence of Nietzsche's time and our own. He proceeded to trace the legacy of the Buddha's social insights across history and to apply them in the present. Mishra has found in the Buddha's spiritual perspective an implicit critique of politics and "progress" in the modern world that for him—as a journalist, an intellectual, and a human being raised in India—have never quite added up.

The Buddha, Mishra says, understood that large-scale political and economic structures could never spell the end of human suffering, or the creation of societies in which human beings genuinely pursued happiness. Alone among social philosophers, the Buddha concerned himself with "a close and dry analysis" of the inner world of experience. And to the helpless people caught in the chaos of his time—as to nineteenth-century thinkers mesmerized by the tumultuous upheavals of theirs—the Buddha spoke with singular clarity. Mishra summarizes: "The mind, where desire, hatred, and delusion run rampant, is also the place—the only place—where human beings can have full control of their own lives."

We cannot control everything and everyone around us, the Buddha taught; we can only control our experience of the world, our perceptions and conclusions in the present, and the way we choose to live. The spiritual disciplines he articulated—meditation, mindfulness, and an embrace of suffering and transience as predictable features of life—make this possible.

As I read Mishra and spoke with him, I thought about how, in the early 1990s, the political scientist Francis Fukuyama created a minor furor when he proclaimed "the end of history." With the fall of the Soviet Union, Fukuyama argued, capitalism and liberal democracy had been vindicated, and the future would be defined by their inevitable, permanent, and peaceful hold. Fukuyama's theory drew criticism and no small amount of scorn. But Pankaj Mishra's eye on the twenty-first-century world brought home to me just how deeply Fukuyama's way of thinking in fact has prevailed. Liberal democracy and market economies are insistently promoted by Western leaders as global panaceas, all evidence to the contrary notwithstanding.

Mishra found echoes of the Buddha's perspective on the spiritual shortsightedness of this approach even in leading thinkers of the Enlightenment, such as David Hume and Adam Smith. Smith's 1776 treatise, *The Wealth of Nations,* launched the doctrine of capitalist political economy and free enterprise. It is the foundation of Western economic thinking to this day. Mishra discovered that just a few years before his most famous work, Smith himself spelled out the human cost of capitalist progress—and the contradiction and implicit cynicism in the economic theory he was about to unleash on the world. I am stunned when I look at these reflections from Adam Smith's *Theory of Moral Sentiments* of 1759:

> The poor man's son, whom heaven in its anger has visited with ambition, admires the condition of the rich. It appears in his fancy like the life of some superior rank of beings, and, in order to arrive at it, he devotes himself forever to the pursuit of wealth and greatness. Through the whole of his life, he pursues the idea of a certain artificial and elegant repose, which he may never arrive at, for which he sacrifices a real tranquility that is at all times in his power, and which, if in the extremity of old age, he should at last attain to it, he will find to be in no respect preferable to that humble security and con-

tentment which he had abandoned for it. Power and riches appear, then, to be what they are, enormous machines contrived to produce a few trifling conveniences to the body. They are immense fabrics, which it requires the labor of a life to raise, which threaten every moment to overwhelm the person that dwells in them, and which, while they stand, can protect him from none of the severer inclemencies of the season. They keep off the summer shower, not the winter storm, but leave him always as much and sometimes more exposed than before to anxiety, to fear and to sorrow, to diseases, to danger and to death.

This is a reflection on human nature—not theological but spiritual in the deepest sense—a revelation of paradox at the heart of a thinker whose theories underpin U.S. culture today.

I'm surprised and then again not when Pankaj Mishra tells me that the theologian Reinhold Niebuhr is one of the thinkers he admires. Niebuhr called democracy an art of "finding proximate solutions to insoluble problems." He was a passionate advocate of democracy, but he warned that we had based our vision of democracy's supreme good in human life to social structures particular to the modern West, especially a robust middle class. From a very different time and place, Mishra echoes Niebuhr's overarching theology that warned at every moment of the temptation of hubris in human life. Our highest ideals and our greatest accomplishments, he said, would always be mixed with the frailty of human nature and our corresponding capacity for incomplete vision, overreach, and self-deception.

I'm committed as a journalist to political neutrality. More operative in me, however—and to similar effect—is a kind of Niebuhrian awareness of the nuance and temptation to hubris present in human nature on every side of history and politics. So, for example, I'm profoundly disturbed by the language of "collateral damage" which has been invoked most recently by a Republican administration. But I hear it as a symptom of a larger tendency, across the liberal-conservative spectrum in this country, to describe our enemies as less than human. Since shortly after the 9/11 attacks, the notion of "hunting down" terrorists has become accepted lingo. In Abu Ghraib, tortured prisoners were posed as animals. Those soldiers and commanders were unconsciously emboldened, I am sure, by language of less-than-humanness that has become routine in our political life and on the pages of liberal as well as conservative papers of record. And yet this mode of attack is doomed to failure, certainly against our current enemies. "You can't outhate a fundamentalist," Yossi Klein Halevi says. "They will win."

A military chaplain, Major John Morris, sat across from me in a radio studio in 2006 in full battle camouflage after his second tour of duty in Iraq. He described one of the most awful days of his service in Fallujah. He stood before the charred body parts of four American contractors hanging from a bridge across the Euphrates. Fury consumed him, along with a certainty that the people who did this did not deserve to live. They were animals. He would be the agent of God, the wrath of God. As that conviction seized him, he understood that he was at an abyss that would render him capable of the very actions he hated. "God help me and have mercy on me," he prayed. "Save me from becoming a debased, immoral human being, and save my soldiers as well." Prayers like this, theology like this, belong in our common life.

I return to a theological long lens—a theistic context, if you will, for the Buddha's social philosophy—that I took from one of my Collegeville conversations with a wise New Testament theologian looking back on life. Paul Minear, I had heard from others, wrote great theology that was never known by the masses. I have never forgotten a pivotal idea he left me with, nor until recently have I quite known what to do with it. He tells me that as he has grown older, he has sought to see political and religious events and institutions with a radically different vision. He wonders, could we begin to see the world, to see history, as God sees history? What would it mean to participate in what is truly important, and to ignore what is truly distraction?

I find that altogether odd and unsettling things happen to my vision as I struggle to see and hear the merciful, reconciliatory heart of religion despite riveting, better-publicized rancor. This angle of approach to the broken world resists choosing sides and accepts antithesis and contradiction as given realities much of the time. I find that I grieve as bitterly for the broken humanity of the perpetrators of crimes as for their victims. I excel at righteous indignation, full of loathing for self-serving people who behave destructively and arrogantly in the name of faith. But I find it harder and harder to label and dismiss them, render them abstract. I am constrained to be mindful of both the fragility and the resilience of the human spirit. I sense that seeing the world the way God sees the world means, in part, grieving in places the world does not forgive, and rejoicing in places the world does not notice. It would mean, therefore, to live with a patience that culture cannot sustain, and with a hope the world cannot imagine.

CHAPTER FIVE

EXPOSING VIRTUE

WHEN I FIRST INTERVIEWED PEOPLE ACROSS the Christian world, I began to imagine religious truth as something splintered and far-flung for good reason, too vast for one tradition to encompass. I saw reformers across time as people who noticed a scattered piece of the Christian truth that the church itself was neglecting. They picked it up and loved its beauty, and saw it as necessary, and embodied its virtues. The Anglicans saw common prayer, Lutherans saw the Bible, Mennonites saw pacifism, Calvinists saw intellectual rigor, and the Quakers saw silence. And the multitudinous traditions I haven't named in that inadequate summary see nuances of those pieces of truth and other aspects altogether, all of which make the whole more vivid, more possible, in the world. This analogy holds as I now explore the splinters of all of the world's traditions. The gentle singlemindedness of Zen complements the searching discipline of Theravada Buddhism. The exuberant spirituality of Sufism rises to meet the daily lived piety of Sunni and Shiite Islam.

But truth and beauty interact with human frailty. In the eternally reenacted motifs of Genesis, light intertwines with darkness. The shadow side of my tale of a world of scattered truth is that as soon as human beings pick up a piece of the truth, they make their mark on it. They codify and literalize. They distort the rest of the picture to fit their chosen center. This happens with every version of truth, surely, in politics as well. But religious truth, flattened out, becomes an especially blunt instrument when it enters the political theater of debates and power plays—a weapon with the same transcendent power religion has to inflame hearts, to infuse life and death with meaning.

There is a difference, of course, between religion and spirituality, and some say that "religion" alone is what complicates our political life. Religions would be the containers of faith—containers malleable and corruptible in the hands of the people who fashion and control them. Spirituality would be faith's original impulse and essence. I appreciate this distinction and at the same time am wary of drawing it too starkly. Religious traditions are bearers of manifold beauty and a weight of human reverence across time. They sustain disciplines and rituals human beings crave as much as they crave raw encounters with the divine. From our first breath, we need structure and routine as deeply as we delight in mystery. In some mysterious way, "containing" religion helps to unlock the sacred within us. It enables us to participate in the human encounter with the divine even when our own spirits are dry. Even in those times, we can say the words and sing the songs and find courage in them, borne along by the hope and trust and company of others.

A rabbi, Sandy Eisenberg Sasso, gave me the best illustration I know of the difference between spirituality and religion. On Mount Sinai, she says, something extraordinary happened to Moses. He had a direct encounter with God. This was a spiritual experience. The Ten Commandments were the container for that experience. They are religion. I find this example wonderful because it gets precisely at the wrong way religion is often taught, and the way it enters politics through words and positions. We proclaim and pass on the rules. We divorce them from the sweep of the spiritual history by which they were discerned—a history that tells of an incomplete and ever-evolving human capacity to comprehend the nature of God and the ultimate meaning of religion. By the time Moses had carried the commandments all the way down the mountain the first time, his people had begun to worship a golden calf.

The Croatian American theologian Miroslav Volf makes a distinction between "thick" and "thin" religion, drawing on the analytical categories of sociology. This is a helpful corollary and underpinning for Vincent Cornell's description of "radically superficial" Islam. I have found Volf's analysis supremely useful as I navigate conversations about religious and political realities and possibilities. "Thin religion," as he describes it, is not religion lacking in zeal. It is religiosity reduced to a formula, and this can render the passion behind it very dangerous.

> It's religiosity reduced to a single symbolic gesture. And once you reduce religion to that . . . you can then project everything that you want onto that. So you believe in one God who is one, who is all powerful and who is also *for* you. And suddenly you've got this immense servant to do all the dirty work that you need to be done and for yourself to feel good as that has happened. [Thin religion] isn't textured. It doesn't have depth.

It doesn't have relief. It doesn't rely on the long history of that religion with all the varieties of reflections that have gone on in the religion. It doesn't even rely on a full understanding of the sacred writings of the scripture.

Volf identifies the dynamic of "thin religion" in a place like Rwanda, where faithful churchgoers—people who were there every Sunday—took up machetes against their neighbors. He knows it most intimately and describes it most vividly from the Balkans, where he grew up. He was teaching in Croatia as the former Yugoslavia broke apart amid the ruins of the former Soviet Union, and violence in the name of God flared as it has many times in that part of the world.

During the war in former Yugoslavia you could occasionally see a Serbian fighter sitting in a tank and flashing three fingers. And those three fingers represented, believe it or not, the Holy Trinity. Flashing that sign meant, "We Serbians, we know how to cross ourselves." Now, clearly he was making a religious statement, but what kind of religious statement was it? It was a religious statement as a marker of cultural identity. It was a religious statement as an indicator of his belonging to a particular group that has a particular religious history. It was maybe some indication that he wants to do something with that religion, but that is a very thin religiosity. Thin religion is manipulable.

Thin religion lends itself to crisis and violence that make the news. Traditional investigative journalism excels at exposing vice—the tail end of a definitively failed struggle with light and darkness. The complexity, paradox, and gentleness of thick, lived religion can elude the calculus of politics and journalism. But I'm out to investigate thick religion. I'm out to expose virtue.

I return again and again to the problem of language. Words that connote religious virtue and morality in our culture are freighted by partisan overuse and popular cliché. *Love* is so watered down as to be practically unusable. *Peace* smacks of unreality and *justice* of vengeance and *humility* of ineffectuality. *Compassion* sounds noble but obscure and possibly naive. Phrases like "ecumenism" and "interfaith understanding"—necessary antidotes to the sectarian violence that permeates the news—describe exacting pursuits and laudable goals that many in our world long for. But they can sound generic and abstract, too broad and too safe. They do not begin to convey the edifying, life-giving nature of those pursuits for those who follow them. *Edifying,* by the way, is an underused word that I love. Virtue and morality are intriguing and thrilling when seen at work in all their complexity. Kindness—an everyday by-product of all the great virtues—is at once the simplest and most weighty discipline human beings can practice. But it is the stuff of moments. It cannot be captured in declarative sentences or conveyed by factual account. It can only be found by looking attentively at ordinary, unsung, endlessly redemptive experience.

As a journalist I'm deeply aware of how strangely tricky it is to make goodness seem relevant, or at least as perversely thrilling as evil. Our culture's lens of perception is a mirror image of the mystical vision of Julian of Norwich. As perpetually horrified as we are of terror and brutality and war, we are riveted by them and we let them define our take on reality. The communications miracles of the twenty-first century make wondrous connections possible, and yet they also bring us images of horror with an immediacy and vividness that are debilitating. Violent images seem altogether more solid and substantial, more decisive and telling, somehow, than kindness, goodness, and lived peace. It is easy to bow down before these images and give in to the despair they preach.

But if I've learned anything, it is that goodness prevails not in the *absence* of reasons to despair but *in spite* of them. If we wait for clean heroes and clear choices and evidence on our side to act, we will wait forever. And my radio conversations teach me that people who bring light into the world wrench it out of darkness and contend openly with darkness all of their days. So the environmentalist and Nobel Peace Prize laureate Wangari Maathai is credited with the astonishing, heartwarming accomplishment of helping to plant thirty million trees. But she has fought governments and industrialists and a bitter ex-husband in the process. Now she is a minister in a new Kenyan administration that was to reverse a history of corruption, and it is mired in corruption scandals of its own. Wangari Maathai's grace and wisdom are won through all of this, not despite it. Mother Teresa, Mahatma Gandhi, Martin Luther King Jr., Dorothy Day—none of them were simple, unsullied heroes in a storybook way. They were flawed human beings, who wrestled with demons in themselves as in the world outside. For me, their goodness is more interesting, more genuinely inspiring, because of that reality. The spiritual geniuses of the ages and of the everyday don't let despair have the last word. Nor do they close their eyes to its pictures, or deny the enormity of its facts. They say, "Yes, *and* . . ." And they wake up the next day, and the day after that, to act and live accordingly.

Sometimes complex virtue sheds its light in entire societies. As the Cold War division of Europe disintegrated, it felt miraculous that at the same time half a world away, the apartheid regime of South Africa was also unraveling. Like the Berlin Wall, apartheid had seemed the shape of reality. *Miracle* is a word the venerable Archbishop Desmond Tutu used to describe the peaceful transformation of his country. Just as wondrously, South Africans then set about naming the moral evil in their history and addressing it directly. As the Truth and Reconciliation Commission was conceived, I recalled Elie Wiesel's words to me in Berlin that changed world ago—his realization that it could be as difficult to be a child of those who ran the concentration camps as a child of those who died in them. The complex moral tragedy of the Holocaust—the human waste of its victims as well as its perpetrators—was not addressed by the Nuremberg trials that brought Nazi leaders to account. This was a classic Western-style process of judgment and punishment, with no eye toward redemption. The most memorable existential comment it yielded was the philosopher Hannah Arendt's numbing declaration of "the banality of evil."

I've spoken with architects of South Africa's process of

truth and reconciliation. They do not claim to have accomplished collective redemption. Their country continues to struggle with the everyday difficulty of the human condition and with manifold legacies of a century of structural brutality. Among the hardest truths they acknowledged was the paradox described in Genesis—how incestuously pain and pleasure, vice and virtue, mingle in every human life. They called black activists to account for crimes in the name of liberation as well as the white leaders of the old apartheid regime for crimes in the name of control. They sought to avoid the irony of every successful revolution: victims of oppression all too easily become perpetrators themselves. They engendered clarity on this fact as a source of preventive vigilance. South Africa's new leaders also relearned the ancient lesson of the importance of time. Truth can be told in an instant, forgiveness can be offered spontaneously, but reconciliation is the work of lifetimes and generations. Toward that, they did what they could in the here and now. They planted risky, constructive, edifying seeds for their society to move forward on a different footing. They gave common people as well as new leaders and former villains accessible resources for moral reckoning. The notion of *ubuntu,* a piece of African philosophy, helped make the Truth and Reconciliation Commission possible. *Ubuntu* augments and adds to our common store of vocabulary for deep moral virtue in the world. Loosely translated, as South Africans have explained to me, it suggests *humanity*. It says, I *am* through you and you *are* through me. To the extent that I am estranged from another person, I am less than human.

I'm sometimes part of conferences or panel discussions where "virtue" and "morality" and "character" are addressed almost as abstractions. How can we define such things in a pluralistic society, the questions begin, and how support them? These conversations always only come alive when people start telling stories—stories of children changed by adults who care; of groups of colleagues making a difference in a particular corporate culture; of role models and teachers and friendships that altered perspectives and lives. Human relationship—which begins with seeing an "other" as human—is the context in which virtue happens, the context in which character is formed. It is an elemental piece of truth, against which individualistic American culture struggles, that we human beings need others from our first breath—at first to stay alive and in the end to be alive in spirit.

Miroslav Volf puts a finer, harder point on this: we are substantially defined not only by those we love but by who our enemies are. Our own identities are shaped by our interactions with them. As a Croatian Protestant, he was defined by the identity and convictions of Serbian Christians. We are all, whether we wish it or not, in profound relationship with our enemies, especially when that relationship is a combative one. When we respond in kind to hatred and aggression, we risk becoming like our foes. And so the biblical virtue of "love" of enemies is not romantic but practical, a love of action and intention, not of feeling. This religious wisdom would subvert the either/or choices often presented for debate in our age, where rhetoric about enemies local and global abounds. This faith requires both realism and compassion. We might need to fight our enemies or keep them at a safe remove; but we cannot let hatred, anger, and fear toward them determine our character and our actions. This cleansing of focus is the true purpose of forgiveness.

I am repeatedly amazed at such clear-eyed instincts of faith—and how they stand in spectacular contrast to faith's current reputation for meanness and smallness. Clear-eyed faith asks me to confront my failings and the world's horrors. It also demands that I search, within all wreckage, for the seeds of creativity, wisdom, and strength. It frees me to see the contours of virtue alive in the world—of "thick" religion, grounded and refined in practice and thought, text and tradition, and responding in differentiated ways to human reality. I come across it, vigorous in far-flung lives and particular communities, in likely and unlikely places, every day, every hour.

One of the phrases that recurs most often in my interviews—in Jewish as well as non-Jewish voices—is the moral longing and commandment to "repair the world," *Tikkun Olam*. There is a Jewish legend behind this notion. Sometime early in the life of the world, something happened to shatter the light of the universe into countless pieces. They lodged as sparks inside every part of the creation. The highest human calling is to look for this original light from where we sit, to point to it and gather it up and in so doing to repair the world. This can sound like an idealistic and fanciful tale. But Dr. Rachel Naomi Remen, who told it to me as her Hasidic grandfather told it to her, calls it an important and empowering story for our time. It insists that each one of us, flawed and inadequate as we may feel, has exactly what's needed to help repair the part of the world that we can see and touch. Religious traditions offer up stories like these as practical tools to a world longing to address images of suffering that can otherwise overwhelm us. Our public life needs moral vocabulary like this as much as it needs sophisticated vocabulary for political, economic, and military analysis.

The clear-eyed faith I find alive in the world also wants to be more searching and articulate about what is really at stake in the moral ideas we turn into political issues. And it suggests that if we do so, religious perspectives should soften the tenor and progress of our common grappling with con-flicted issues, not harden them. One of the most helpful conversations I've conducted, many listeners tell me, was with two evangelicals on opposite sides of the gay marriage issue. Richard Mouw and Virginia Ramey Mollenkott are two devout, learned individuals who love the same Bible but have come to very different theologies of sexuality. Richard Mouw, who does not believe that the church should sanc-tion same-sex marriages, has nevertheless spent a great deal of time in conversation with gay and lesbian people. He's come in himself to something he calls "sexual humility." This is the kind of language that I believe could reframe some of our hardest debates and put them on a new footing. He tells this story:

> I heard a minister once stand up at a meet-ing, a very conservative minister, and he said, "I think *we normal people* ought to say to these folks . . ."—and I just wanted to scream, "You're normal? Let's have a medal for the one normal person in the room!" I mean, normality doesn't come easy in all of this. And there's so much else that we have to admit we're broken people about. I just wish we could lower the rhetoric on this and

really talk about who we are and in the broader cultural debate, where we really want to go with all of this and what our real fears—what are the hopes and fears that go into all of this—rather than just ideologically trading rhetoric.

Virginia Mollenkott came out as a lesbian thirty years ago, publishing "Is the Homosexual My Neighbor?" To Richard Mouw's proposal of sexual humility she adds her own longing and challenge that—on both sides of the gulf of opinion on gay marriage—we attempt to speak "from the holy in ourselves to the holy in the other."

Such language stirs my imagination about what a religious approach might add to our collective soul-searching on gay marriage and other political divides. Just as strikingly, it insists that the task of being Christian in this debate is about more than the policies one advocates. The way we approach our divisions, Mouw and Mollenkott suggested with one voice, is as telling a reflection of the substance of our faith as the positions we take. Religious perspectives like this won't change minds overnight, nor make some of the large questions before us simpler. But they can enable us to engage and honor the humanity of different others. They can make a new kind of conversation possible.

A South African scientist, George Ellis, a cosmologist and a Quaker, makes the fascinating proposal that there are basic ethical principles built in to the very fabric of the universe, in the same mysterious but certain way that the laws of physics are embedded. Ellis had professorships in Italy, the United States, and Germany, before returning in the 1970s to apartheid-era South Africa, his homeland. There he became passionate about promoting social change. He used mathematical models—effectively—to critique social injustice. At the same time, he used his advanced understanding of the cosmos to think about the power of human behavior. He began to take seriously the way human emotions, choices, and actions drive cause-and-effect in the physical universe. And as he experienced dramatic social transformation in South Africa, he came to believe that there is such a thing as "the true nature of deep ethics." We don't invent mathematical truths, like pi or $E=mc^2$, he points out. We discover them. The same can be said of the ethic of self-giving and self-sacrifice that he experienced at the heart of radical, peaceful change in South Africa. The fact that every major spiritual tradition expresses some version of this ethic and its attendant virtues—humility, patient endurance, compassion—counts for Ellis as a scientist as a roundabout form of proof. In this way, we can reimagine religious people and spiritual thinkers as explorers. They are practitioners of a kind of science of virtues, preserved in traditions that speak in many languages and address the reality of each generation anew.

Our world of fluid movement and communications is connecting ethical and spiritual innovators—the explorers of our time—in ways that have not been possible up to now except on the level of a Mahatma Gandhi and a Martin Luther King Jr. and a Rabbi Abraham Joshua Heschel. People often ask me where I see the counterparts of these great visionaries in our time. Where, for that matter, is the Niebuhr of our day? Surely Desmond Tutu counts, and Thich Nhat Hanh, and Mother Teresa. Niebuhr belonged to an American culture in which a white Protestant Christian male voice could have a primacy and privilege unimaginable and undesirable now. I think the Niebuhrs of our day are to be found less in the spotlight and more at work locally, regionally, within religious traditions and outside and across them. Public theology in our time must be a far more dispersed, plural, multifaceted, and multiply articulated thing. Globalization's dark side is widely publicized, its destructive and destabilizing potentials documented. But at the same time, globalization makes possible a new kind of arms-open human embrace of difference. Religion hinders this in places, yet it profoundly facilitates it in others.

The Salvadoran American scholar Manuel Vásquez has a special interest in what he calls the "little religions," local practices and beliefs by which human beings navigate the opportunities and dislocations of the global era. He tells me that this focus on "lived religion" gives him a nuanced and essentially hopeful sense of what globalization will mean for human beings. He also says that most Americans have no idea how U.S. culture will be changed by religious and spiritual worldviews we are now importing. He and his colleagues are involved in long-term studies of the impact on both sides of the flow of human beings between Latin America and the United States. He's studying Mayan immigrants—marginalized peoples even in the culture they come from—to wealthy retirement communities in Florida. He's watching Salvadoran Californian gangs and the global Pentecostal networks that have arisen to minister to them. These are not the immigrants of old, who left their homes behind and assimilated. They are transnational, maintaining deep roots in several cultures; globalization makes that possible. And religious rituals, convictions, and communities play a defining role on every side of this equation. Manuel Vásquez says: "Religion is one of the best vehicles to deal with both the local and personal and also the global and the universal. Religions have been doing this for centuries. They have universal messages of salvation and very personal strategies for coping with chaos."

We tend to focus on the economic and the political

when we speak of globalization, but Manuel Vásquez speaks of the present as a time of "the globalization of the sacred" as well. I see this too. Most positively and counterintuitively, globalization's tools of communication and connection magnify the potential force of individual lives of virtue and communities of care. Local vision and practice are beamed out to far-flung places. African women planting trees in their villages to revitalize the ecosystem; volunteers around the world caring for the poor and building schools and hospitals; doctors and nurses treating the injured of war; young people redefining interfaith dialogue in Chicago; bankers and community leaders innovating microeconomics in Bangladesh—all are part of vast globalized networks of practical care. These "saints" of every tradition are rarely famous, but they are living lives of meaning and they are repairing the world they can touch and see. It remains for the rest of us to see and honor the vigor of such efforts, their undeniable reality, their force in and beyond the fluid mystery of time.

And again, how we look for them will make all the difference. News reports about human need and suffering can achieve the opposite effect that journalists and advocates who present them intend and desire. Litanies of statistics, for all their usefulness as public policy tools, turn people and pain into numbers—numbers unfathomable to reckon with, too awful to contemplate in any detail. I hear how many children around the world will die tomorrow for lack of clean water, how many children got up hungry this morning—and inwardly I throw up my hands in despair. I feel helpless against all of that; it is painful and abstract at once. I cleave to the simple manageable care I can give my own children at home tonight.

When Hurricane Katrina hit New Orleans in the summer of 2005, it temporarily broke the self-protective dam many of us had erected between the blight of poverty in the United States and the semicontrolled havens of our own lives. Terrible images came into our living rooms of one hundred thousand New Orleanians, mostly African American, who were too poor to evacuate the city and were then left to fester in subhuman conditions. The director of the Federal Emergency Management Agency was quoted as saying, "We're seeing people we didn't know existed." This awakening echoed across our nation. How can it be, commentators asked, in the richest country in the world, that so many residents of the core of New Orleans were invisible even to authorities. And how did the rest of us become isolated from their despair?

I was helped in those days after Katrina by conversation with a physician, David Hilfiker, who enabled me to remember forward about the collective history by which poverty and racial isolation formed at the heart of American cities. Two decades ago, he gave up his medical practice in the Midwest and moved to inner-city Washington, D.C. He was driven more by spiritual questions than by religious answers, but was drawn to the idea that God is somehow revealed in the poor. He and his family joined an unusual faith community, the Church of the Savior, that stresses both contemplation and action. Over the past fifty years, the Church of the Savior has innovated a web of sustainable local responses to poverty, mostly in the poorest area of Washington's Adams-Morgan neighborhood. Dr. Hilfiker and his wife, Marja, helped to found a medical shelter for chronically ill homeless men who were turned away by hospitals. They lived with three other doctors and their families above the shelter, called Christ House, in community with their patients. Later he and his family founded Joseph's House, a supportive residence for homeless men with AIDS. Dr. Hilfiker came to a personal sense of a mysterious and pervasive religious idea that all of our spiritual well-being is somehow "wrapped up" with the poor.

Yet he found himself immersed in the ghetto without any idea how such places had come to be common features of American cities. He undertook straightforward historical research and published a small, startlingly commonsense pamphlet, laying out with clarity how concentrated centers of poverty and racial isolation came to form in urban centers across the United States. The story David Hilfiker discovered is rich with good intentions and with irony. In the last half century, dozens of federal programs—programs that raised many other Americans out of poverty—systematically disadvantaged poor African Americans. For example, the original Social Security Act signed by Franklin Delano Roosevelt in 1935 excluded domestic and agricultural workers—fields in which two-thirds of black Americans were employed at that time. The Federal Housing Administration, created in 1934, brought many post-Depression Americans into the middle class by helping them get mortgages, but this same government program redlined most black neighborhoods as too risky. In the same way, federal urban renewal all the way through the 1970s created subsidized housing, but it concentrated the poorest people more tightly together. And the federal interstate highway program connected most of America, but as a side effect, it often divided or decimated the poorest African American neighborhoods. The problem, as David Hilfiker points out gently and eloquently, is that the same Americans who were invisible until after the hurricane hit have been invisible for a long time, stranded and isolated even by the march of progress.

Knowing this history helps me. It reveals this terrible injustice as the consequence of a string of human mistakes and shortsightedness, but not as a faraway conspiracy impossible to comprehend or untangle. And Hilfiker gives me some vocabulary of word and action—building blocks of virtue—that help me think forward and beyond my complicity in this. He makes a helpful distinction between "charity" and "justice." Charity is something, he says, over which we have control and that we do in a profound sense for ourselves. He does not condemn charity, and he considers the work of his life to fall mostly into this category. But we must also find new ways to pursue justice—to engage the structures that make inequities possible and perpetuate them. Justice makes charity less necessary.

David Hilfiker's children were eleven, nine, and four when they first moved to Washington. I find his descriptions of his children's response to living with poverty as helpful as anything he relates. Like many parents, I turned off the worst images of despair from New Orleans, afraid of the fear and despair with which they would fill my son and daughter. Counterintuitively, Hilfiker insists, our children will be better able to live constructively with the fear and pain of poverty in our world if they are not merely shielded from it. This is true, of course, of every kind of pain and darkness that intersects our lives. And he describes manageable first steps in the here and the now: that we venture out, with our children, and put human faces and stories to the poverty closest to us now. Because of the deep segregation that defines our urban centers, middle-class and affluent people literally don't see their poorer neighbors, can't easily recognize them as neighbors in the first place. Relationships can break our paralysis by giving us concrete ideas of what structures need reforming. This resonates with everything I learn in my life of conversation. The great virtue that makes every virtue possible is human relationship, *ubuntu*, humanity.

As much as I have protested that virtue alive in the world is not about lovely platitudes, beauty is one of its defining attributes. A passion for beauty has always been at the core of human religious experience. Art, architecture, literature, and music owe everything to religion. The examples begin pouring out if you ponder this for just a second, lush and wild: not just the music of Bach, but the mandalas of Tibetan Buddhism, the calligraphy of the Qur'an, and on and on and on.

It was a Muslim thinker who put a theological point for me on this link between beauty and essential spiritual virtue. Khaled Abou El Fadl has put his life on the line, as the title of one of his books puts it, "wrestling Islam from the extremists." But when I sat down with him for a public dialogue with a rabbi, Harold Shulweiss, in Los Angeles, I wanted to draw out gentler words I'd noticed throughout his writing. He insists that the key to the future of Islam lies in recovering its "core moral value of beauty": God delights in beauty, Islam teaches at its core, and is beauty. Beauty is in creation, not destruction. It is in the human intellect and the human heart, El Fadl goes on to infer, and in their powers to apply sacred text toward creation, balance, and knowledge in the deepest sense. Like other Muslims I've spoken with, he finds an underpinning theme in the Qur'anic teaching that God created humanity male and female, and of diverse peoples and tribes, "so that you may come to know one another."

That night in Los Angeles, Rabbi Shulweiss responded in kind, recalling the evocative Jewish biblical counterpart: "the beauty of holiness." This is a beauty of wholeness, he said—not just of forms and shapes but of relationships. It contradicts the fractionalizing force of religion, which after all was invented by human beings, not by God. We talked that evening about some of the bitterest issues in modern life: why religion gets us into such trouble, why religion paradoxically is at the heart of so much violence and war. Often when religious people are asked to speak of such things, they begin with doctrine, or ethereal ideals like moral imperative or divine justice. Our conversation drove to high places that night but by a different route—to another kind of critique these religious men, a Jew and a Muslim, could make of actions done in the name of religion. Is it beautiful, or is it ugly? This question was proposed as a theological measuring stick, a credible litmus test. Does this action reveal a delight in this creation and in the image of a creative, merciful God who could have made it? Is it reverent with the mystery of that? Khaled Abou El Fadl is intense and brainy, a professor of law at UCLA, and on this night he was nervous. But he mesmerized his audience at a Jewish cultural center as he relaxed and spoke out of his passion for his faith:

> Beauty is to fall in love with God, to fall in love with the word of God, with the Qur'an, and to feel that it peels away layers of obfuscation that I have spent numerous times building around myself. Beauty is to look around me and fully understand and feel therein is God, in all I see around me, and to understand my place in this. That I am integral as God's viceroy, as God's agent on this Earth, like everyone else. And at the same time, that I am wonderfully irrelevant. . . .
>
> We try to capture in a word—you know, we say God, we say Allah, we say whatever word. But it is beyond language, and it's something that those who have experienced

can attest to it, but those who have not are
puzzled by it. I celebrate [God's] love in living and in my ecstasy in seeing life. I do not
engage in a lot of activity that other people
enjoy—for instance, going skiing or playing
hard American football. But the joy in
watching all of that, in honoring it, is overwhelming. It's an overwhelming passion and
an overwhelming truth.

This is religious virtue infused at once with a sense of
cosmic purpose and with humility; irrepressible, vivid with
grace, anything but banal.

Eyes and ears to see beauty, to attend to poverty, to seek
justice—these strong, recurrent biblical themes are often
missing from our public discussions about "moral values."
But I know from my life of conversation that they are tended
in countless lives. And I'm hopeful that voices from the vast
middle might coax new life in the coming period into our
collective awareness of such virtues. I've said in the introduction to this book and I'll state again here, uncategorically,
that virtue is not the exclusive domain of religious people.
Religious assertion misrepresented and abused can be far
more amoral than an absence of religion. And there is a

range of groups in our time—the ethical culture movement, nontheistic universalists, pagans, to name just a few—cultivating edifying, life-giving communities and practices without reference to God.

I'm also fascinated when I see "secular" voices rediscovering core religious ideas and giving them a new interpretation and life in our culture independent of the traditional institutions. The journalist Bruce Feiler is a cartographer of the new geographic/spiritual realities of life in the post-9/11 world. A lifelong secular Jew, he had traveled to sixty countries and sprained his ankle on four continents but had never been to the Middle East. Then in the late 1990s, he visited a friend in Jerusalem and was astonished to find the biblical stories attached to concrete places he could touch and see and feel. In March 2001, he published a life-changing, bestselling book, *Walking the Bible*. "The objective of that experience and in some ways the destination of that experience," he told me, recounting a truth that he himself articulated with great surprise, "was that the Bible is not an abstraction, that book gathering dust. It is a living, breathing entity, intimately connected to those places and to all of us."

In ways Feiler could not have foreseen, his discovery of the power of religious stories came to mirror a journey he believes American culture as a whole has been on, especially since 9/11. On that day, he watched the twin towers fall from the windows of his apartment in New York. And in the weeks that followed, as the questions began—Who are they? Why do they hate us?—he heard one name echoing: Abraham. He sensed that at its root, this crisis had to do with religions kindred by genetic spiritual ancestry. The conflict between "the Muslim world" and "the West" and Israel—a transposition of an age-old recurring conflict between Islam and Christianity and Judaism—is a family feud. September 11, Feiler says, is the day the Middle East came to America. Yet all three of the monotheistic traditions claim Abraham—a fully human figure—as a common ancestor on the way to knowing God. Abraham is central to Jews and Christians and arguably most central to Muslims.

Feiler's intriguing proposition—one with enormous potential and practical relevance, I believe—is that biblical stories themselves have a power that predates and transcends the way religions have flattened and used them against each other. But there is no simple, straight path to that happy outcome. Feiler went looking for Abraham as a figure that might bring the world together—a hero in the desert, a great oasis he could unveil to the world. He found not one reconciliatory Abraham, but hundreds of competing versions of Abraham and his story. "Most of my waking hours were spent trying to untangle this knot," Feiler says. "How the universal figure of Genesis who spreads his blessing to everyone becomes this object of bloody rivalry among his descendants."

The trajectory of Abraham is fascinating, and it crisscrosses crises and dynamics of the present age. In what would have been somewhere between 2100 and 1500 BCE, it is written that Abram was born in Ur of the Chaldeans, southeast of present-day Baghdad. He settled in a desert outpost in modern-day Turkey. There, when he was seventy-five years old, the Hebrew Bible says that God spoke to Abram and he responded. He turned his back on the idol worship of the ancestors who came before him. He worshiped one God and in so doing became the original, iconic monotheist, though in fact the Zoroastrians of that same part of the world may have preceded him. In the biblical account, Abram and his wife, Sarai, traveled through lands that mark the political landscape of today: modern-day Syria, Jordan, Egypt, and finally to what we now know as the West Bank.

But Sarai was barren. The Hebrew Bible recounts that when Abram was ninety-nine and Sarai ninety, God told them they would have a child. He renamed Abram *Abraham,* a word that in the Hebrew suggests "the father of a throng of nations." Sarai was renamed Sarah. And in the kind of whimsical moment in the Bible that I love, the name of their firstborn son, "Isaac," means in Hebrew, "he laughs"—for Sarah laughed and imagined herself the object of laughter when God gave her a child in old age.

Isaac would become the father of Jacob, who would become Israel. But Abraham had another, earlier son, Ishmael, born to an Egyptian slave, Hagar. The world's 1.2 billion Muslims consider Ishmael their original ancestor and their line of direct descent from Abraham. And when Christianity grew from Jewish roots, one of the core messages of the early apostles was that Gentiles too could become children of Abraham.

With a real-world story, Bruce Feiler brings this biblical drama into the present for me with a hope that is at once countercultural and pragmatic:

> One of the last things I did is I went to Hebron, one of the bloodiest cities on the planet, the epicenter of Muslim-Jewish conflict. I drove south on this sniper road where the Israelis and Palestinians shoot at one another before arriving at the Tomb of the Patriarchs. It's this giant building that looks like a cross between a gymnasium and a castle. The last time I had been there, there were ten thousand Jews dancing in a festival.

Today it was empty. It was so dangerous that four soldiers with helmets and machine guns had to escort me inside. Four!

And I go to this little tiny room between Abraham and Sarah's tomb. All three faiths agree this is where they're buried. There's a ramshackle synagogue there with a chandelier hanging down with half the bulbs out, and it's there that Abraham, at age 175, dies. And in one of the most haunting and overlooked passages in the Hebrew Bible, in Genesis 25:9, his sons Ishmael and Isaac—rivals since before they were born, estranged since childhood, leaders of opposing nations—come to stand side by side and bury their father. Abraham achieves in death what he could never achieve in life: this moment of reconciliation, a hopeful side-by-side flicker of possibility where they're not rivals or warriors, Jews, Christians, or Muslims. They are brothers.

What I think is relevant here is that this is also a Muslim shrine; it's been a Muslim shrine for hundreds of years. Muslims and Jews now divide the shrine. In some ways, the shrine is sort of an awkward but really practical model for how you can get along. It ain't pretty. Jews and Muslims, they split the shrine and ten days a year each side gets unlimited access to it. It ain't pretty, but it does work. And maybe that's the model here. But what's important to me about that [biblical] moment is that they stand side by side. It doesn't say they hugged. It doesn't say they had dinner. It doesn't say they moved in and sat down and said, you know, "Let's forgive." And remember, Abraham had tried to kill each of them. To me, that is the model. And, again, the text seems to understand—predict, almost—where we're going to be so many thousands of years later. So the destination here is not some Esperanto mumbo jumbo of a giant religion. It's standing side by side and respecting that coexistence.

Feiler and I have a lively exchange about what it means to treat this kind of biblical story as relevant apart from the traditions it gave rise to. Since he published his book *Abraham* in 2002, Abraham discussion and action groups have sprung up across the United States. He says, "I believe that the stories contain an enormous amount of truth that is still relevant to my life and to most people's lives that I know. That really matters to me. And what I find myself doing is trying to go around the religions or go behind the religions, back to the initial story." I counter that Feiler and others wouldn't have the stories to find meaningful if religions hadn't retold them, preserved them, and propelled them forward in time. But he wonders if this is not just a function of the story of Abraham, for example, being so "true" and so great that it has survived the pummeling and distortion it took by religious people all these centuries.

Still, this story represents for me an irony and paradox at the heart of the spiritual energy of our age—and the complex relationship spirituality and religion have in ways both good and bad. Even as people go back to ancient texts to find meaning the traditions haven't given them, they tend to rediscover the virtues the traditions themselves originally formed around. They rediscover the power of sacred text and story, the need for community to explore and live out these teachings, the power of ritual to commemorate them. In coming back to religion by first going around it, some are reinventing and invigorating its deepest virtues for new generations and a changed world.

CHAPTER SIX

CONFESSING MYSTERY

———

PEOPLE ASK ME ALL THE TIME how my own faith has evolved and how it changes through this life of conversation about ultimate things. I find that a daunting question. I started to write this book to give it the textured, lengthy answer it deserves. On some level the longer I do this work, the curiosities I began with—the human pursuit of meaning and mystery, the nature of God, the contours of faith, the point of religion—grow so large and rich that generalizing words have ceased to touch them.

In my early life, I longed for solutions and systems and overarching themes that would bring meaning into focus and apply to all people and all places. The people with whom I spend my life of conversation now are eloquent, but with infinite variety of emphasis and description. Each in his or her own sphere of experience and influence has grappled with the contradictions between power and love, fear and hope, that first began to haunt me in Berlin. I enter into their worlds and meet them with questions. If it is a good conversation, we are both surprised by what we hear and what we give voice to. Something magical happens in a real conversation, where people bring the clearest words they can muster, and the most natural, to matter and meaning. Paradoxically, what is most personal also lands in other ears as most universal. What we have to say takes on an importance larger than ourselves. This happens just as palpably when I experience that "something larger" to suggest a presence of God, and the other person does not.

The changes this works in me are not seismic but subtle. My conversation partners describe a slice of the variegated human apprehension of mystery and how they pin it to their piece of earth. I stay tethered, like it or not, to my piece of earth. I have continued to commune with books as much as with people for my private confusions and solace. I am kept grounded by the ordinary, often exhausting, always life-giving demands of mothering my children. I am raising them in the same spectacularly interesting and unsettling world from which some take refuge in contained religious worlds. I understand that. I'm frightened too at times and precisely when I'm intrigued by the wonders of the world I'm often out of my depth. I cleave to faith's capacity to yield to questions and to comfort, even as certainties unravel. I have had to apply the exacting virtue of forgiveness, including forgiveness of myself, where it seemed laughable, unbearable. I've known the failure of hope and the failure of love in these years of my life since I discovered theology—a struggle with clinical depression, and the end of my marriage to Michael.

Sometimes I have had a feeling—and I had this in my marriage to Michael—that God throws out the occasional wild card, almost a dare—try this if you will; I will bless it; it is rich with possibility; it will not be easy. And in the case of my marriage, Michael and I failed to carry it through to the end. We lost the dare. That might sound like I experience my marriage as a mistake, and that is most definitely not the case. Our amazing children are the best proof of the blessing, the real sacrament, that grew from our marriage. But the children are not my only proof by far. Together we embarked on a theological adventure that has brought me to what I do now, what I feel I am supposed to be doing in this world.

So what does this mean? What does it say about *providence,* a weighty Christian word with all kinds of resonance in American culture and Christian theology? What does it mean when what feels like vocation emerges from the wreckage of what felt like grace? I am now divorced, a word I never thought would apply to me. I did not go into my marriage lightly, and it ended only after years of struggle to repair the brokenness between us. It ended with the end of hope, I suppose, and a conviction that God would not require me to live permanently with disrepair at the center of my life. These years onward, Michael and I have learned to honor and love each other practically as parents to our children.

My depression came a year after our arrival in Minnesota—a year in which, for the third time in a decade, I had completely changed lives, worlds, roles. It was triggered by the pressures of change and exhaustion, but like much depression it reflected at bottom old, old sadnesses suddenly grown unbearable. I learned to perform, and to survive, growing up in my family, but I did not learn enough about love. I had all the classic physical symptoms of this epidemic malady of body, mind, and spirit. I stopped being able to sleep. I lost weight at an enormous rate. I was dulled and eventually paralyzed by fear and a sense of hopelessness.

Ignatius Loyola, the sixteenth-century founder of the Jesuit order, spoke of "desolations"—a better word than depression, in my mind—that "lead one toward lack of faith and leave one without hope and without love." For me, depression was not so much about being without faith or hope or love; it was, rather, not being able to remember knowing those things, not being able to imagine ever experiencing them again.

Medicine pulled me out of the depths of numbness and despair. But only a slow, uneven climb back through time, and into truth, has brought me to a place where I could begin to sense the abundance of life and hold fast to it. In therapy I learned in a more than academic and aesthetic sense how active memory—and eventually an awareness of the past lived with and chosen—can truly burden and enliven the present. And I learned how I needed the certainty of hope offered—a future I could not feel, but a future that I trusted to show me the meaning packed away inscrutably in belabored days of darkness. Joy eluded me for some time, as did any lasting experience of relief. But I was making discoveries that would coalesce into wisdom. I was seeing things I would not have looked for in easier times. With time I have come slowly, fitfully, to accept my depression as a gift, albeit a black Pandora's box that nearly swallowed me. I needed to engage its cautions and perils if I were to become whole and wholly myself. That is not to say that this life with more memory, more of my consciousness of the failure of love, is not hard. It is hard and, paradoxically, joy when it comes is fiercer.

As I pulled through my depression, I was moved anew by how wise the Bible is, how psychologically savvy. Again the Hebrew scriptures provided the inside-out comfort of mirroring the messy breadth of human reality, of the difficulty of the struggle for human integrity within the context of a longing to know God. In particular now I came to an appreciation of the Psalms' insistent and often combative cries about "enemies"—something that had previously repelled me and alienated me from praying anything but selectively. I now knew enemies internal as well as external—experiences and wounds with the power to haunt "my sleeping and my waking." I could now pray a line like this and pray it fervently:

> For my enemy has sought my life
> And has crushed me to the ground;
> Making me live in dark places
>
> My spirit faints within me;
> My heart within me is desolate.

As I live beyond depression and divorce—and yet live with these realities as part of the story of who I am forever now—I am helped by my ever-deepening understanding that faith as a whole encompasses and blesses human vulnerability. It took years, even after I had apprehended this idea intellectually, before I thoroughly internalized its implications in my own life. The perfectionist in me is strong, and at first I approached spiritual challenges much as I had approached the Cold War. But gradually, I have been able to understand healing, like faith, as paradoxical, most effective when it incorporates what is broken rather than denying or curing it. I learn from a recovering alcoholic, Basil Braveheart, when he speaks of living sober for thirty years because he has, in Lakota tradition, taken alcohol as his teacher and his family. I learn from the physician Rachel Naomi Remen, not a religious figure per se but a kind of quiet modern-day mystic, that the way we deal with the losses of our lives, large and small, may be what most determines our capacity to be present to the whole of our lives; we burn out not because we have stopped caring, but because our hearts are too full of grief. My divorce and my depression are losses I must know and feel and integrate. They make me a better interviewer and human being, more present to the world and its hardest realities.

Those hard realities—the problem of theodicy, the failure of love on the largest possible scale—and the concomitant consequences of endless, needless suffering in the world, do not become less troubling with time. Even as I learn new vocabularies of sense and wonder I continue to find that suffering too has imponderable variation. I learn not to imagine that beautiful words and lives will somehow snuff out what is dark and difficult. Again and again I am fatigued by a sense of powerlessness at injustices and atrocities close to home and far away. I have seen too much. But religious traditions give me language and ideas to hold on to ambiguity—the pleasure and pain of human experience that complicate and enliven each other at their depths. I have this redemptive exchange with Dr. Remen, who speaks to these dilemmas of the human condition through her experiences as a doctor:

> We thought we could cure everything, but it turns out that we can only cure a small amount of human suffering. The rest of it needs to be healed, and that's different. It's different. I think science defines life in its own way, but life is larger than science. Life is filled with mystery, courage, heroism, and love—all these things that we can witness but not measure or even under-

stand, but they make our lives valuable anyway.

But I ask her, aren't the destructive aspects of life also mysterious and unmeasurable? We can also observe evil. Yes, she concurs, that's certainly true, then adds, "But, you know, the issue is not to eradicate evil. I'm not sure evil can be eradicated. I think it's part of the human condition. The issue is to commit yourself to what's important to you."

This kind of journalism I do is, as much for myself as for others, about looking beyond the horrors of the evening news to the redemptive stories that are not being told, to ways of being in the world that keep sense and virtue and the possibility of healing alive in the middle of the world's complexity.

As I finished writing this book, I spent time in a monastic room at Saint John's Abbey in Collegeville, where my adventure of conversation started. The monks gather five times a day for prayer on an ancient cycle—morning, noon, daily communion, evening prayer, compline. My favorite time to join them is evening prayer. As the day draws to a close, they chant and recite cycles of psalms, alternating between the pews on each side of the altar. The abbey church was constructed in the 1960s by the avant-garde architect Marcel

Breuer, and it works as a vast echo chamber. It is as though we send the psalms back and forth across the church and to each other.

One of the most exacting periods of this writing was made excruciating for me by news of bombs sending devastation across the Lebanese-Israeli border. The pain of my Israeli and Palestinian conversation partners was once again made current, and relevant, and layered with a new set of grievances and consequences. And in the fixed abbey cycle of prayer, on days in which the news was filled with the Lebanese city of Tyre in ruins, there appeared lines about long-ago war and friendship between Tyre and the ancient Israelites. These lines were too heavy with real-time blood and tears for me to pray them with any comfort. I forced myself to mouth them, along with the others, along with the generations who prayed them before me. I have learned to pray the whole spectrum of psalms—including the violent and wrathful psalms about enemies, and the entire genre known as imprecatory or "cursing" psalms—as an act of presence with those many people in the world at any given moment whose experience of real threat and fear and fury is all-consuming.

And then several weeks later, I was in the abbey church again when a young monk stood up to read that evening's assigned lesson. It was a passage from the Song of Solomon, one of those books whose inclusion in the canon delights as many as it confounds. This love poetry, I felt, metaphor for divine love or not, was not designed to be recited solemnly by a celibate man as a piece of set liturgy. But we listened earnestly as he bravely uttered lines about "rounded thighs like jewels" and "breasts like two fawns, twins of a gazelle" and "kisses like the best wine that goes down smoothly"—and sat down again. I was struck, as I often am in that church and others, by the strangeness of what we do there. This recital of sensual passion made the liturgy more unworldly. And more wonderful. I had to hide my smile of compassion for the young monk and of pleasure.

The mess and mystery of the physical is something my conversations teach me to better incorporate into faith, like the range of emotions dark and light that define us. Becoming wiser about spiritual things for me has meant learning to live in my body, not just my head. Denying the vigor and fullness of our bodies, as puritan Christianity did, renders us as incomplete as if we stopped praying. Other traditions do a better job with this. Judaism's prayers bless intricate bodily functions in elaborate detail. Muslim prayer is full-body prayer. Eastern Orthodox Christianity, as its gorgeous liturgies aspire to evoke heaven on earth, celebrates the sensual as a manifestation of divine grace and transcendence.

And not coincidentally, I believe, the varieties of Christianity that are exploding most rapidly around the world are Pentecostal and charismatic. A quarter of the world's Christians—something like half a billion people and growing, outside the traditional Christian denominations and across them—are part of the Pentecostal movement that began just a century ago on Azusa Street in Los Angeles. This is a great untold religious story of our time. And it is full-body religion, as a Roman Catholic Pentecostal sociologist, Margaret Poloma, first helped me see. Pentecostal worship is marked by bodies swaying, ecstatic music, hands lifted and waving, bodies prone and rolling on the floor, spontaneous tears and prayer, laughter that seems to come from deep inside the body, and language with no earthly translation. Poloma calls this a form of mysticism—"main street mysticism"—with some precedence in ancient Greece as well as the African spirituality of many of Pentecostalism's founders. Charismatic Christianity contradicts the post-Enlightenment culture and religion that distanced themselves from the physical and emotional catharsis that religious ritual used to provide communally and individually. Protestants centered their religious lives around "a lecture" and squeezed the faithful into pews where they had to sit up straight. They even squeezed religious ritual, music, and theater into this setting. Of her studies of charismatic movements in the United States and abroad, Poloma says:

I truly believe that we as human beings are wired in such a way that we do require [cathartic] responses—not only emotional response, but even physical responses. And I think at one time, certainly religion could provide that. It certainly does in other cultures, but in our own culture, much of our faith is an intellectual exercise, particularly for those of us who are more scholarly. We'll make it a matter of belief: "Does it make sense?" "Is it rational?" When this kind of a movement happens, it doesn't even make sense to ask those kinds of questions. So I ask different questions. I try to look at what is the role that the physical body might play in releasing some stress. What role does catharsis play in our well-being?

In 2006, five of my producers and I traveled to Azusa Street in Los Angeles to the global centennial gathering of the Pentecostal movement. It was moving to vicariously experience this spiritual energy that has spread across the world since it was unleashed there a hundred years ago. Pentecostals emerged from the Holiness movement, insisting that Christians should claim the "gifts of the spirit" as sources of spiritual power to face the challenges within themselves and in a changing world. As described in the Bible, those gifts or *charisms* include teaching, preaching, healing, prophecy, wisdom, and speaking in tongues. Speaking in tongues became a kind of initiation and litmus test for Pentecostal faith. I was most struck on Azusa Street by the improbable mix of humanity that Pentecostalism has the capacity to touch and empower. The three-year height of the original Azusa Street revival drew people of all classes and races under one roof when that was nearly unthinkable—and under African American leadership. Some Pentecostal churches were ordaining women a half century or more before today's most liberal Christian denominations. Like every human revolution, this one has struggled to retain its own highest ideals. Black, white, and Latino soon often worshipped apart. Nonetheless, a complex global mix of rich and poor was on display in Los Angeles again in 2006, a lavish juxtaposition of skin colors and cultures. The transformative power of their whole-body spirituality was palpable.

The founder of the Azusa Street revival, William J. Seymour, once said, "We are not fighting men or churches but seeking to replace dead forms and creeds and wild fanaticisms with living, practical Christianity." In such words, one hears the appeal of Pentecostalism in his time and in ours. Across the world, Pentecostalism has a special appeal for people at the edges of society, authority, and religion. It is often emancipatory for women. It has a demonstrated power against social ills that are compounded by poverty, such as the dissolution of families, and the destructive force of addiction. One of Margaret Poloma's most striking findings, for me, is that ecstatic experiences in charismatic worship seem to translate back in real life to a deepened capacity to love oneself, one's spouse, one's children, one's coworkers. Pentecostal activists have created programs of care in the poorest, most dangerous neighborhoods in U.S. cities and around the world. This religion seems to bear out a truth of one of my least overtly religious interviews, with a lovely man, Matthew Sanford, a paraplegic who is an expert practitioner and teacher of yoga. He has observed that the more completely we live in our bodies, frail and fallen as they may be, the more compassionate we become toward all of life.

Over time I've grown into a sense of my vocation as described in a line of the writer Annie Dillard: "You were made and set here to give voice to this, your own astonishment." I first read Dillard at divinity school. When I rediscovered that line early in my radio adventure, I was hoping to interview her for a program on the difference between "faith" and "religion." I talked to a Buddhist teacher, Sharon Salzberg, who was happy to use the word *faith* generously, wanting to redeem it for wider use than conservative American rhetoric. I talked to a rabbi, Lawrence Kushner, who told me that the word is really only used by Christians, but then proceeded to give me one of the loveliest definitions of "speaking of faith" that there will ever be: "It pushes the edge of language. One of the reasons that speaking of faith is such a slippery and a moving target is because we're trying to talk about the stuff of which we are." But Annie Dillard turned me down. She was working on a manuscript, her publicist said. Someday I will get her, and I look forward to that.

So to console myself I take out my marked-up copy of her beautiful, wildly spiritual, barely comprehensible memoir/reflection, *Holy the Firm*. It is a weekend, one of my weekends away from my children, and I am alone. The passage I am searching for—a definition of faith that survives in memory years and years after I first read it—is on a page that I find torn corner to corner, two ragged halves. It was torn by my love for the beauty of words and what they can convey. Here it is:

> Faith would be that God is self-limited utterly by his creation—a contraction of the scope of his will; that he bound himself to time and its hazards and haps as a man would lash himself to a tree for love. That

God's works are as good as we make them.
That God is helpless, our baby to bear, self-
abandoned on the doorstep of time, wondered at by cattle and oxen. . . . Faith would
be, in short, that God has any willful connection with time whatsoever, and with us.
For I know it as given that whatever he
touches has meaning, if only in his mysterious terms, the which I readily grant. The
question is, then, whether God touches anything. Is anything firm, or is time on the
loose?

I think all the time about what Annie Dillard is
describing—this baffling concreteness and randomness we
experience even as we discern there is an ultimate order.
Maybe physics, not theology, will resolve this puzzle for
us—which is why I have to keep interviewing scientists all
along the way. Maybe the largest part of what I am doing is
simply grabbing people—this scientist here, that rabbi there,
this secular New Yorker who discovered he had a soul in the
midst of mental breakdown—and asking them to tell me
what they saw, what they glimpsed however fleetingly. Because however fleeting, these "glimpses" are transformative.
They stay with you, long after you can still remember clearly

what you saw and even begin to doubt that you saw it, and they work on you from the inside. The shared glimpses of others stay with me, changing the way I move through the world. But my work of questioning and seeing and knowing and unknowing and living remains mine to do. I did not really know, when I first delighted in Annie Dillard's lyrical musing on faith, how hard life could become. When I read it now it is less lyrical and more true, even painful to take it in its supposition: God is self-limited by his creation, that is to say in some infinitesimal measure by me.

In another place in *Holy the Firm,* Dillard recalls that in Hebrew myth angels belong to nine different orders, the highest being the seraphs, who are aflame with love for God. Cherubs, who are second, merely possess perfect knowledge of him. "So love is greater than knowledge," she writes. "How could I have forgotten?" I did not mark this passage with my red pen when I read it ten years earlier. I forget that love is more important than knowledge all the time. I have forgotten it, willfully, for long stretches of life, and at my peril. Yet even as the loves in my life are in disarray I recover a sense of its centrality. And every time I let myself go deeper into the mess and mystery of human loving, I am hit over the head again by theology—an insistence that the love of God is so much fuller than we can usually imagine or take in, just like those glimpses I try to get people to describe for me. I keep pursuing faith, if for no other reason than because it is the place in our common life that keeps reminding us of the necessity of love—not the romantic love of poets, but the practical love of the sacred texts—however fraught and imperfect our practice of it may ever and always be. The desert fathers and mothers offer this supreme and practical comfort in the face of our culture's confusions: love is not the starting point but the goal. It is not something we are born knowing how to do, not something we fall into. It is something we spend our whole lives learning.

I hold as one of my favorite writings in the world a paragraph by Reinhold Niebuhr about love—as an impossible yet necessary ideal in the lives of nations as well as human beings. It appeared in his book *The Irony of American History.* His daughter Elizabeth Sifton took it as the epigraph of her book about her father, and it ended *Speaking of Faith*'s program on the legacy of Niebuhr's thinking for our time:

> Nothing that is worth doing can be achieved
> in our lifetime; therefore, we must be saved
> by hope. Nothing which is true, or beauti-
> ful, or good, makes complete sense in any
> immediate context of history; therefore, we
> must be saved by faith. Nothing we do,

however virtuous, could be accomplished
alone; therefore, we must be saved by love.
No virtuous act is quite as virtuous from the
standpoint of our friend or foe as it is from
our own standpoint; therefore, we must be
saved by the final form of love, which is
forgiveness.

I was filled with a kind of panic, as I neared the end of this
writing, that I was running out of words. My words were not
numerous enough, not large and lush and gorgeous enough,
not up to the holy and human grandeur and unruliness and
specificity of the slice of life I am trying to put words around.
And of course I was right.

I knew this in the beginning. In the beginning when I
interviewed people, I would always say, Remember, we are
talking about something that is ineffable, trying to put words
around something that will always, ultimately, defy them.
We do our best. But we are left, in the end, with arms full,
minds full, of mystery.

And that is exactly where we must end, and where I
must end, and then continue to let the voices of my show
speak. At their orthodox core, religious traditions themselves
ask us to hold our notions of earthly certainties and tran-

scendent mystery—what we believe we know, and what we can never know for sure in time and space—in an exacting, creative tension.

Mystery is the crux of religion that is almost always missing in our public expressions of religion. It eludes and evaporates beneath the demeaning glibness of debates and sound bites. Mystery resists absolutes. It can hold truth, compassion, and open possibility in relationship. This relationship could redeem our otherwise hopelessly literalistic, triumphalist civic and religious debates. We could disagree passionately with each other and also better remember the limits of our own knowledge. If mystery is real, even more real than what we can touch with our five senses, uncertainty and ambiguity are blessed. We have to live with that, and struggle with its implications together. Mystery acknowledged is, paradoxically, humanizing.

I find that *mystery* is a word people of every tradition love, whether they speak it often or not. It is a word that many nonreligious people are open to embracing and exploring, perhaps more so now than in previous generations. Introduce mystery into any conversation and the conversation gentles; reality doesn't lose its sharp edges but the sharp edges are not all, not the end. Mystery takes form and substance one life at a time, though long ago we learned we could also summon its presence together. Mystery is at the heart of all ritual—layers and layers of idea, liturgy, postures, lifted prayer, constructed to capture and express something that cannot be contained. Mystery is apprehended fleetingly, but it leaves its mark. Our traditions are imprinted and suffused with it, endlessly washed and chastened by it, evocative of its memory, expectant of its return.

Some would say that this is precisely the engine of violence; that religious people can claim to answer only to a wrathful transcendence, released from earthly norms of justice. But fanaticism is more presumptuous, more flagrantly dismissive of mystery, than any degree of nonbelief. Some might say that I'm proposing mystery as a cover for relativism. That taking mystery as a primary value, I leave open a suggestion that all truths are equal, all convictions relative. But I know in myself and in my conversation partners that we are driven to discern truths, each of us with the raw materials of life that we've been given. This is the object of our built-in compulsion to ask who we are and how we got here and how to give meaning to our days. I need to discern my tenets of truth constantly, know their texture, revisit and cleave to their assurances as keenly as I feel how they are changing and expanding as I grow older. But to believe is not to have all the answers; to discern truth is not to be able to carry it all the way to the end. This truth is ultimate: I exist in time and space. We see through a glass darkly, said the ever-confident apostle Paul.

So I can sit with the Vietnamese Buddhist monk Thich Nhat Hanh, who is not a theist, and feel that this might be the closest I will ever come to sitting in the presence of God. Thich Nhat Hanh's counsel has been sought in recent years by CEOs at the World Economic Summit, Harvard Medical School faculty, even members of the U.S. Congress. The practice he describes is basic Buddhism—a set of practices for living more mindfully in the present. It begins with following one's breath as a way to plant oneself firmly in the moment. But Thich Nhat Hanh's teaching is unusually practical in application and lyrical in expression. He is a poet as well as a teacher. He doesn't stress special sitting postures or avoidance of conflict. The retreat where I interviewed him was attended by dozens of police officers, people who carry guns for a living. His counterintuitive message is this: even the most painful and violent experiences of life demand our full attention. When we are attentive to our own suffering, he insists, we will know that of others. That knowledge can help break cycles of suffering and violence in the world around us. Yet Thich Nhat Hanh surprises me when he makes a statement about "the kingdom of God." He could not imagine the kingdom of God to be a place without suffering, he says. For how, then, would we learn to be compassionate? This is a striking Buddhist inversion of the Christian preoccupation with the problem of evil.

In our time, spiritual insights like this offer themselves as disciplines for living for people of many traditions and no religious faith at all. Even Richard Mouw, devout evangelical whose faith irrevocably contains an imperative to convert others, has speculated with me that Christ might appear in times, in places, in whole cultures, in "anonymous" guises. I can't know the accuracy of these ways of thinking, nor do I need to. I know I have to admit mystery alongside, within, religious doctrine. The activist nun Joan Chittister, who was raised with Protestants on one side of her family and Catholics on the other "regularly reprising the Thirty Years' War" is today part of global interfaith projects and networks. She's a founding member of the Woman's Global Peace Initiative, together with a Hindu nun, a Buddhist nun, an Orthodox Jew, an Islamic scholar, and a Protestant clergywoman. She says this:

> The six of us are calling people together, women together, in areas of conflict around this world to be a living sign that no religion, the heart of none of the great religions really supports, endorses, or sets out to pro-

duce war or killing or death for anyone. So what I have learned is that God works in many ways on this globe and that the scriptures of the other have insights for me that basically confirm my own insights. They don't weaken my Christianity or my Catholicity. If anything, it tells me more clearly who I am, but it also tells me, very profoundly and respectfully, who these other people are. If God is one, why would it be so surprising that the six of us would have a oneness in ourselves?

The geneticist Lyndon Eaves tells me that the spirituality of the scientist is akin to that of a mystic: it's a constant endeavor to discern truth while staying open to everything you do not yet, cannot yet, know. It is to live boldly and assertively with the discoveries you have made, all the while anticipating better discoveries to come. It is a life, in that sense, marked by an enlivening, creative humility.

From the beginning of my life of listening, I have observed fierce humility as a quality in the lives of people I admire. But deep spiritual humility defies the connotations of self-debasement, of ineffective meekness, that our culture assigns to the word *humility* and that I too imagined until I dug into sacred text, and lived with my children, and embarked on this odyssey of conversation. Even after I began to study theology and learned to value the great nuances of the New Testament, I was frankly puzzled by the teachings of Jesus that his disciples should become humble like a little child. And then I became a mother of little children.

I know of no richer source of theological enlightenment than parenting. This is the body of raw experience with which I constantly revise and fill my image of God—as father, as parent—with complex meaning. The God of my childhood was sovereign, all-powerful; the real experience of parenting is more often one of excruciating vulnerability. Our love for our children is often defined by the fact that we cannot spare them pain and save them; that we give them their freedom as necessary steps to creativity, wisdom, and love; that we raise them for the world they go on to create. And as I watched my children move through the world, I began to imagine what Jesus meant by humility. The humility of a child, moving through the world discovering everything anew, is closely linked with delight. This original spiritual humility is not about debasing oneself; it is about approaching everything new and other with a sense of curiosity and wonder. It has a quality of fearlessness too, that I first recognized in monastics and have since experienced in a vast far-flung communion of saints of many faiths and no faith at all. Spiritual humility intensifies one's sense of the limits of words about God, of words about mystery, their narrowing possibilities and their vulnerability to distortion by the human frailties even of the institutions created to preserve them.

Nevertheless, we keep speaking, St. Augustine said, in order not to remain altogether silent. I started out this adventure with my grandfather's face—stern and full of maddening contradictions, intelligent eyes bright with humor, and the best he could muster of love. That image, his life, forbade me to write off a religious sensibility I find lacking, a system I have rejected, wholesale. Now my head is full of many voices, elegant, wise, strange, full of dignity and grief and hope and grace. Together we find illuminating and edifying words and send them out to embolden work of clarifying, of healing. We speak because we have questions, not just answers, and our questions cleanse our answers and enliven our world.

INDEX

Abraham, story of, 52, 200–205
Abraham (Feiler), 204–5
Adwan, Sami, 159
African Americans
   poor, 191–93
   and racism in America, 101–2
Ahmed, Leila, 139–40
Al Qaeda, 146, 147, 155
Al–Rahim, Ahmed, 160–61
Alcoholics Anonymous, Serenity
   Prayer, 19
American Public Media, 118
An Ironic Christian's Companion
   (Henry), 125
angels, seraphs, and cherubs, 223
anti–Semitism, 99, 101, 138, 145

apartheid, 180–82
Arabic, 137–38
Arendt, Hannah, 180
Armenian Orthodox, 122
Armstrong, Karen, 14, 42–44, 48,
   140, 141–45
*At the Entrance to the Garden of
   Eden* (Halevi), 157–58
atheist nations, 29
Augustine, St., 232
Austen, Jane, 72
Azusa Street, Los Angeles, CA,
   217, 218–20

Bassett, Paul, 123–24
Beagle Diary (Darwin), 70

Benedictines, 16, 60–61, 117–18, 122, 127
Berger, Peter, 6
Bethge, Eberhard, 93
Bible, 49–54
  Genesis, 61, 62–66, 202, 203
  Gospel of John, 114–15
  Hebrew Bible, 50, 62–63, 116, 201–4
  King James version, 23
  New Testament, 54–60, 114, 231
  Old Testament, 50, 62
  proof–texting, 138
  Revelation, 105–6, 141
  violence and, 140–41
Bondi, Roberta, 14, 128–30
Bonhoeffer, Dietrich, 12–13, 27, 32–35, 49, 66, 92–94, 126
Book of Common Prayer, 54
"Boy Breaks Glass" (Brooks), 150
Braveheart, Basil, 212
Brooks, Gwendolyn, 150
Brother Lawrence, 47–48
Brown, Dan, 56
Brown, Robert McAfee, 124
Brown University, 26–27
Buber, Martin, 96
Buddha in the World, The (Mishra), 164–66
Buddhism, 88, 93–94, 109, 164–66, 228–29
Buzenberg, Bill, 133

capitalism, 31, 37–38
Cathedral of St. John the Divine, 120, 131
Catholic Church. See Roman Catholic Church
Celebration (Spufford), 77–79

charismatic movement, 217–18, 220
children, and "spirit of religion," 68
Chittister, Joan, 125, 134, 229–230
Christian fundamentalism, 152–55
Christian realist, 20
Christian theology, 32–33
Christianity
  charismatic, 217–18, 220
  desert fathers and mothers, 129–30
  early Christians, 119–20, 123
  German, 33–35
  Holiness church, 122, 123–24, 218
  Islam and, 141–43
  Pentecostal movement, 217, 218–20
  Serbian Christians, 182–83
  varieties of, 216–20 See also evangelical Christianity
Church of England, 54
Church of the Savior, 192
clear-eyed faith, 183, 184–85
Cloud of Unknowing (anonymous), 47
Cold War, 5, 7, 28, 75, 145
Coles, Robert, 68
Collegeville Institute, 118–19, 122–24, 126, 128–31, 214
Communism, 30–31, 37
compassion, knowledge acquired by, 42–43
Confessing Church, founding of, 33–34
conservative Protestants, 21–22, 153–57
Copernicus, Nicolaus, 68
Cornell, Vincent, 146

Cox, Harvey, 5
creation, 61–67
    Darwin and, 69, 74
    and science of evolution, 61
Creation and Fall (Bonhoeffer), 49
"cursing" psalms, 215

Da Vinci Code (Brown), 56, 59
Darwin, Charles, 14, 67, 69–73, 74, 88
David, King, 50–51
Davies, Paul, 103, 104–5
Davis, Ellen, 62
Dawkins, Richard, 5
Dean Man Walking (Prejean), 126
Deia (island of Mallorca), 45–47
democracy, 31, 168–69
depression, 209–12
Diekmann, Godfrey, 131–33
Dillard, Annie, 16, 220, 221–23
Dirac, Paul, 85
divorce, 209, 212

Eaves, Lyndon, 87–90, 92, 103, 230
Einstein, Albert, 12, 14, 85, 99–103, 104, 165
Einstein in Berlin (Levenson), 102
El Fadl, Khaled Abou, 148–49, 157, 195–98
Eliot, T.S., 13, 48
Ellis, George, 15, 187
England, 47–48, 49, 54, 58
ethics, 187
evangelical Christianity
    early traditions, 21–26
    politics and evangelical Christians, 5, 135, 154–57
    Protestant and, 21, 153–57

evil
    moral, 94–95
    natural, 77–79
evolution, creation and
    science of, 61

Facism, 33, 99
Feiler, Bruce, 15, 199–205
Feit, Carl, 86–87
first-person approach to religious speech, 126–27
Five Books of Moses, The, 62–63
Fox, Everett, 62–63
Fukuyama, Francis, 166
fundamentalism, 39, 148
Fundamentalism Project, 152–53

Galileo, Galilei, 68, 103
Gandhi, Mahatma, 21, 99, 151, 179
Garner, Jay, 160
Gates, S. James, Jr., 101–2
gay and lesbian issues, 154, 185–86
Genesis, book of, 61, 62–66, 202, 203
genetics, 87–92
Germany
    Berlin Wall, 7–8, 29, 39, 75, 76, 122
    Bonhoeffer's death, 35
    Christian theology, 32–33
    East Germany, 27–30, 75
    Fascism, 33, 99
    Holocaust, 31–32, 96, 180
    plot to kill Hitler, 33, 34
    secular global politics in, 27–30
    West Berlin, 29, 35–40
globalization, 145–46, 188–91
Goldwater, Barry, 5

golem legend, 90
Gospel of John, 114–15
Graham, Billy, 155

Halevi, Yossi Klein, 15, 157–59,
    170
Hamberger, Philip, 163
Harris, Sam, 5
Havel, Vaclav, 7
Hebrew Bible, 50, 62–63, 116,
    201–4
Hegel, G.W.F., 31
Henry, Patrick, 124, 125
Heschel, Abraham Joshua, 151
Hesse, Hermann, 164–65
Hilfiker, David, 15, 191–95
*History of God: The Battle for God,
    The* (Armstrong), 42
Hitchens, Christopher, 5
Hitler, Adolf, 27, 29, 33, 34, 94
HMS *Beagle,* 69–73
Holiness church, 122, 123–24,
    218
Holocaust, 31–32, 96, 180
Holy the Firm (Dillard), 221–23
Hoyt, Thomas, Jr., 125
Hume, David, 166
humility, spiritual, 231–32
Hurricane Katrina (2005), 191–
    192, 194

Iberian Christianity, 123
Immigration and Naturalization
    Act of 1965, 5
imprecatory, 215
Iraq, 160–61, 170
Iron Curtain, 7
Irony of American History, The
    (Niebuhr), 19, 224–25
Islam, 119, 135, 136–39, 141–50,
    175

Islamic Society of North America,
    139
Israel, 157, 158, 159–60, 215

Jacob, 52–53, 202
Jefferson, Thomas, 162
Jerusalem, 158
Jesus, parables of, 57–58
John XXIII, Pope, 123, 125
Johnson, Luke Timothy, 59–61
Judaism, 184
Julian of Norwich, 13, 47–48,
    107, 178

Kant, Immanuel, 31
Keck, Leander, 54–56, 59, 105–
    106
Keillor, Garrison, 118
Kennedy, John F., 4, 5
Kennedy, Robert, 4
Kierkegaard, Søren, 27, 28
King, Martin Luther, Jr., 4, 5, 19,
    21, 151, 179
Kingsolver, Barbara, 82–84
Kling, Bill, 118
Kushner, Lawrence, 221

Lamott, Anne, 127
Lebanon, 215
Leibniz, Gottfried, 74
Lenin, Vladimir, 30
"Letter from Birmingham City
    Jail" (King), 19
Letters and Papers from Prison
    (Bonhoeffer), 93, 126
Letters to a Young Poet (Rilke),
    46–47
Levenson, Tom, 102
liberalism, 39
Lot, 51
Loyola, Ignatius, 210

Maathai, Wangari, 15, 179
Madison, James, 163
Marty, Martin, 152–56, 163
Marx, Karl, 5, 30, 31
Marxism-Leninism, 30
Mattson, Ingrid, 139
Memories of God (Bondi), 128, 130
Merton, Thomas, 13, 58, 110, 116–17
Micah, prophet, 116
Minear, Paul, 170–71
Minnesota Public Radio/American Public Media, 118, 133
Mishra, Pankaj, 15, 164–69
Mollenkott, Virginia Ramey, 185, 186
Moore, James, 73
moral evil, 94–95
Moral Man and Immoral Society (Niebuhr), 19
moral values, 198–99
Morris, John, 170
Moses, 53
Mouw, Richard, 124, 185–86, 229
Muhammad, Prophet, 137, 141–45
Muslims, 135, 136, 137–38, 141–50, 161, 196

narrative theology, 126–27
Nasr, Seyyed Hossein, 61, 147
National Council of Churches, 121, 124–25
National Public Radio (NPR), 133
natural evil, 77–79
natural selection,
Darwin's theory of, 71–72, 88

Nature and Destiny of Man, The (Niebuhr), 19, 20
Nazarene Holiness, 122, 123–24
neurotheology, 88
New Orleans, Louisiana, 191–92, 194
New Testament, 54–60, 114, 231
New York Times, 28, 31
Newton, Isaac, 68, 103
Niebuhr, Reinhold, 13, 18–20, 30, 39, 168–69, 188, 224–25
Nietzsche, Friedrich, 31, 165
Night (Wiesel), 32, 96–99
Nimer, Mohammad Abu, 159
No Man Is an Island (Merton), 116
North African Council of Carthage, 55
nuclear weapons, 28, 37

Old Testament, 50, 62
Origin of Species (Darwin), 69
Oslo Peace process, 157, 158, 160
Ozick, Cynthia, 90

Palestine, 158, 159–60, 215
Palmer, Parker, 14, 126
parables, 57–58
Patel, Eboo, 149–52
Paulist order, 125
Pelikan, Jaroslav, 124
Pentecostal movement, 26, 217, 218–20
Perkins, C. T., 22–24
Philoxenus of Mabug, 129
Piercy, Marge, 90
poetry, religion and the art of, 41, 43–44
Poisonwood Bible, The (Kingsolver), 82–84

Polkinghorne, John, 79–82, 93, 107
Pollack, Robert, 94–95
Poloma, Margaret, 16, 217–18, 220
poverty, 191–95
Prejean, Helen, 126
progressive Islam, 139
Protestants
    Catholics and, 120–21
    conservative, 21–22
    and fundamentalist Christians, 153
    resistance to Fascism, 33–34
    and violence against Catholics, 119–20

Qur'an, 141, 151
Qur'anic Arabic, 137–38

Rauschenbusch, Walter, 21
religion
    and the art of poetry, 41, 43–44
    as center of world affairs, 9
    differences between faith and, 220–21
    first-person approach to religious speech, 126–27
    foretelling the end of, 5–6
    globalization and, 188–91
    language and communication in, 177–79
    "little religions," 188–89
    mystery as crux of, 226–27
    not taken seriously, 6
    religious violence, 139–43, 147–50
    science and, 12, 67–73, 74, 81–93, 99–105, 187–88, 230

scientia of compassion, 42–43
    and spirituality, 173–75
    thick and thin religion, 175–77
Remen, Rachel Naomi, 16, 184, 212, 213–14
Revelation, book of, 105–6, 141
Rhode Island, 26
Rilke, Rainer Maria, 46–47, 111, 164
Roman Catholic Church
    Catholics and fundamentalist Christians, 153
    Catholics and Protestants, 120–21
    Second Vatican Council, 5, 118, 123, 125
    violence against Catholics, 119–20
Rowley, Coleen, 93

Safi, Omid, 137, 139
Saint John's Abbey, 117–18, 214–15
Salvation Army, 124
Salzberg, Sharon, 220–21
same-sex marriages, 185–86
Sanford, Matthew, 220
Sarah, 201–2, 203
Sasso, Sandy Eisenberg, 174
science, religion and, 12, 67–73, 74, 81–93, 99–105, 187–88, 230
scientia of compassion, 42–43
scientia sacra, 61
Scopes Monkey Trial, 73
Second Vatican Council, 5, 118, 123, 125
Secular City, The (Cox), 5

Seemi Ghazi, 137–38
separation of church and state, 162–64
September 11, 2001, religion in post–9/11 world, 9, 42, 93, 94, 95, 135, 136, 199–200
sexual humility, 185, 186
Seymour, William J., 219
Sharon, Ariel, 158
Shulweiss, Harold, 195–98
Sifton, Elizabeth, 224–25
silence, 45
Smith, Adam, 166–67
Social Gospel, 21
Sodom and Gomorrah, 51
Solidarity movement (Poland), 7
Song of Solomon, 215–16
South Africa, 180–82, 187
Southern Baptist, 6, 21
Soviet Union, 4, 29, 30, 39, 176
Speaking of Faith (radio program), 62, 126, 128, 156–57
and difference between faith and religion, 220–21
early idea for, 133–36
Niebuhr and, 224–25
Spiral Staircase, The (Armstrong), 48
spiritual humility, 231–32
spiritual virtue, 195–98
spirituality, religion and, 173–75
Spufford, Margaret, 77–79, 93, 112
Stransky, Tom, 125–26
suffering, magnitude of, 74–80, 107
Sufism, 137
suicide bombers, 147–48

Talmud, 86, 90
Tantur Ecumenical Institute, 125
technology, fundamentalism's use of, 154–55
Terkel, Studs, 131
terrorism, 39
theodicy, 74–76, 212–13
Theory of Moral Sentiments (Smith), 167–68
Thich Nhat Hanh, 16, 93–94, 228–29
thick and thin religion, 175–77
Third World, 39
Tikkun Olam, Jewish notion of, 184
time, perception of, 103–4
Time magazine, 5–6
Tippett, Michael, 47, 113, 208–9
Tocqueville, Alexis de, 161–62
track–two diplomacy, 152
tree of life, 71–72
truth and reconciliation process, South Africa's, 180–82
Tutu, Desmond, 21, 180

ubuntu, 181–82, 195

Vásquez, Manuel, 188–90
Vatican II, 5, 118, 123, 125
Vietnam War, 4
virtue, spiritual, 195–98
Volf, Miroslav, 15, 175–77, 182–83
Voltaire, 75

Walesa, Lech, 7
Walking the Bible (Feiler), 199
Washington, D.C., 192–94

Wealth of Nations, The (Smith), 166–67

Wiesel, Elie, 13, 31–32, 90, 95–99, 180

Williams, Roger, 26

Woman's Global Peace Initiative, 229

women, Islamic, 139–40

Women and Gender in Islam: Historical Roots of a Modern Debate (Ahmed), 140

Writings of the New Testament, The (Johnson), 59–61

Zoloth, Laurie, 90–92

A PENGUIN READERS GUIDE TO

SPEAKING OF FAITH

Krista Tippett

An Introduction to
Speaking of Faith

In *Speaking of Faith*, Krista Tippett offers readers an intimate memoir of her own spiritual journey. Yet this book also serves as an instructive and original guide to discussing the mysteries of life and the meaning of religion in our time as they relate to subjects as diverse as science, love, virtue, and violence.

Tippett's personal story begins in the Southern Baptist culture of Oklahoma, where she first witnesses the power of faith in her preacher grandfather. Fleeing this tradition, she attends college at Brown University and finds herself at home in a demonstrably secular world. She becomes fascinated with the defining global drama of the late twentieth century, the division of the world between capitalism and communism. She is captivated by Germany in particular—one nation torn between east and west. She becomes a political journalist reporting on both sides of the Berlin Wall, and then enters a Cold War side door to diplomacy, working closely with a U.S. ambassador who is a nuclear arms strategist. In this milieu of great power, she begins to question "the limits of politics" where the human spirit is concerned. She enrolls at Yale Divinity School, and later becomes a religion journalist and the host of the immensely popular public radio program *Speaking of Faith*.

Tippett weaves insights from these episodes of her life with wisdom distilled from her "life of conversation" with people across world traditions. The way we speak about faith matters profoundly, she demonstrates, and can help us live differently, across the spectrum of our beliefs, with the great crises and challenges of our time. She illustrates a literate faith that engages mind and spirit together, and grapples imaginatively with questions that touch us all: How do faith and science, religion and politics intersect? Where is God when people suffer? Why do we cause others to suffer in the name of our gods? What is virtue and where is it found? How can we cultivate it—or expose it when we see it? How can we speak unreservedly of the ideals we hold most dear in ways that honor and respect difference?

Speaking of Faith meets those questions and suggests fresh possibilities for framing and addressing them. It invites readers to reflect on the intersection of religious ideas and real life in their own experience, and to join Tippett's ongoing dialogue with wise voices of the past—such as Dietrich Bonhoeffer, the heroic pastor who was executed by the Nazis; Reinhold Niebuhr, the most important American theologian of the twentieth century; and even Charles Darwin, author of "the last classic scientific text to engage theology directly;"—as well as with the diverse contemporary voices on her radio show. Her conversation with the independent scholar Karen Armstrong reminds us that reading theology should be like reading poetry. Biblical scholar Luke Timothy Johnson instructs us, as he vividly puts it, to see these texts not as a cadaver to be examined but as a living body to dance with. The Buddhist monk Thich Nhat Hanh revealingly asks how we would learn compassion if not for the existence of suffering. These wise insights have deeply moved Tippett and are only a few of the many more contained within *Speaking of Faith*. This innovative spiritual memoir is sure to become a touchstone in our nation's ongoing conversation about faith.

ABOUT KRISTA TIPPETT

A journalist and former diplomat, Krista Tippett has created, hosted, and produced the popular *Speaking of Faith*, which has been running as a weekly public radio program since 2003. She lives in St. Paul, Minnesota.

A CONVERSATION WITH KRISTA TIPPETT

What do you hope this book will accomplish? Are there ideas in Speaking of Faith *that are better expressed in book form than on radio?*

Radio is a wonderfully intimate medium, and I always feel that I am conducting my conversations on behalf of and together with my listeners. But I'm in those radio conversations as a journalist, primarily as a listener. With the book, I show my hand. The conversations I have with my guests are powerfully revealing, and I felt that I had a kind of obligation to do this—to trace the line I ask my guests to trace between religious ideas and real life. Writing the book was also an occasion for me to stand back—in a way that is not possible in the thick of a production cycle—and reflect on what I learn and how I see the world differently because of my adventure of radio conversations. As for what the book might accomplish, I am delighted when people tell me it helps them find their own way out of the rut "speaking of faith" has fallen into in our culture. And that is ultimately about far more than words and ideas. In my experience, when we trace the intersection of religious ideas and human experience together, we also learn how to walk that line more imaginatively and practically together.

4

With the possible exception of PBS's Religion and Ethics Weekly, *I can think of no other radio or television program quite like* Speaking of Faith. *Were there any broadcasting models—past or present—that inspired you to create the show?*

I was compelled to create the show because there were no broadcasting models! I emerged from my theological education and found a black hole where intelligent conversation with and about religion needed to be in our public life—a conversation with all the nuance and variety this aspect of being human has in real twenty-first century lives. However, I would say that Bill Moyers paved the way for what I do, with his courage and innovation in taking on large, hard subjects of human spirit and meaning. The enduring popularity of his work emboldened my sense— our entertainment-oriented culture notwithstanding— that there is a great hunger in our time for deep and searching discussions that defy sound bites and simple answers.

Your maternal grandfather looms large in this memoir. If he were alive today, what do you think he would say about your radio program or your book?

I hope that he would be able to see how much the spirit of my work—my desire to pursue the truth and mystery of God—is consonant with the passions that drove his life. I hope that he would see that even an orthodox Christian faith and a biblical theology must be resonant and vital and compassionate and fearless in responding to the insights of a globalized world. If he worried about my doctrine, I hope he would honor my insistence that we must bring our deepest religious virtues to bear as we inhabit this world with different religious and nonreligious others, whatever our theology. And I hope that he would experience what I write about him as a testament to the passion and humanity I love in my memory of his faith, and the fact that they form me even today.

You mention your work as a diplomat. While you found the work spiritually troubling, it seems to have helped prepare you for your role as a radio moderator. Do you think this is an accurate statement? Do you ever think you could have accomplished as much or even more as a diplomat?

I am constantly amazed at how every element of the disparate experiences of my young adulthood came together in the work I do today. I use the skills and instincts I gained as a diplomat all the time as I learn about and interact with people of far-flung religious vocabularies and perspective.

You show many compatible elements among the world's major religions. Do you think there are vital ways in which they are irrevocably incompatible and, if so, do you think peoples of incompatible faiths can coexist peacefully?

I think that, ironically, some of the most basic things we have in common can also divide us most elementally. The fact that many of our traditions share a belief in God and a reverence for sacred text—these can be the hardest places to begin our approach to others because their particularities are so close to our identities. But as I try to say and show in many different ways throughout the book, we might approach each other with new freshness and possibility through the practices and virtues that underpin our traditions and echo across them: hospitality, mercy, mindfulness, compassion, love of neighbor, love of enemy, kindness. Our culture and my fellow journalists tend to define religious people by what they "believe," but our traditions at heart are really far more about how we act, who and what we love, how we live our lives. There's been great hand-wringing in our public life in recent years over politicians and others being "too religious." But how do we judge that—by how stridently they invoke the name of God, or the rightness of their positions on issues? Our public life would not be polarized but enriched and gentled if we began to ask religious people to be genuinely religious—that is to say, true to the core of their traditions, which have mercy and humility front and center, and demand "faithfulness" as much in how we treat those with whom they disagree as with the positions we hold.

Since your book was first published, there has been a flurry of anti religious books, e.g. Christopher Hitchens's God Is Not Great, *Sam Harris's* Letter to a Christian Nation, *Richard Dawkins's* The God Delusion, *and Daniel Dennett's* Breaking the Spell. *Do you think this is marking a return to the secular days of the sixties and seventies? Do you think such books contribute in any way to our understanding of religion and faith?*

These kinds of books and ideas are saying nothing new. They are a twenty-first century version of the "God is dead" mantra of the 1960s that has surfaced cyclically since the Enlightenment and even before. Despite this recurring theme, religion is as visible and vital a part of global life now as it has been at any time in living memory. These books are a kind of counter reaction to that. They rightly name and decry some terrible excesses in the name of religion in our time. But in overgeneralizing about all religious people, they verge on parody. Most ironically, to me, they mirror the stridency—an unwillingness to incorporate evidence contrary to one's fixed opinions—of religious fundamentalists. My bottom line is we have to learn to take religion more seriously, not less so, to understand its force in human life and the world. And for every strident and violent voice that throws itself in front of cameras and microphones, there are countless others leading lives of humility and beauty and good works. We have to look for them to begin to see and hear the whole story of religion in our time. In my book I try to distill some of the creativity and wisdom and beauty I find those kinds of religious people contributing to all the important dynamics of life in our time—from global conflicts to scientific discovery to personal ethics at home and at work. And real change and ferment—meaningful corrective to religious excesses—will only come from these kinds of people, from inside religious traditions themselves. If we don't create spaces to strengthen religion from its center, its dangerous edges will only become more powerful.

The journey that you chronicle is essentially one from politics to religion. It's interesting to note that it is the exact reverse of that taken by many activist fundamentalists in this country. Since at least the Reagan years, Christian activists have been going from the pew to the voting booth with sweeping results. Do you think there is a real threat to our country's division of church and state?

I passionately resist doomsday scenarios. Such ideas have engendered a fear that has embittered and calcified our public life these last years. I see my program and this book as a kind of antidote to that. I try to illustrate the important distinctions between "fundamentalism" and "evangelicalism" and "Pentecostalism," labels that are too often deceptively conflated by journalists and others. I think one of the most important contributions *Speaking of Faith* has made to the journalistic landscape about religion in recent years is to present a nuanced view of Evangelical Christianity—which has long comprised about 40 percent of the population, a vast swath of human beings. My memory of my grandfather's complexity and contradictions and humanity has driven me forward in this as well. And the evolution that has taken place within Evangelical Christianity in part in reaction to the experience of political power—has been rapid and remarkable. There is a new generation of evangelical leaders adding issues like climate change and global poverty to their moral values agenda. I'm following that.

Have you had any extraordinary conversations since writing the book that you would like to share with your readers? Are you contemplating a sequel to this book?

I'm often asked to cite my favorite interview ever—but my favorite interview is usually the last one I had! In the months since I published the book I've interviewed a delightful acoustic biologist who reflects on her Quaker spirituality by way of her study of the songs of whales and the calls of elephants. I've interviewed an Armenian Orthodox theologian/master gardener and a Hindu physicist. Many of our listeners were also taken with a delightful conversation I had with Shane Claiborne, who is part of a fascinating new movement emerging from Evangelical Christianity called "the new monasticism." These young people are unimpressed, as they say, with "the narrow agenda of conservatives" and the "shallow spirituality of liberals." They're not sure Jesus would recognize what goes on in the churches they grew up in, and they are connecting the dots between local need and global crises. This kind of imaginative faith—that is wise and bold and pragmatic at once—keeps me doing this work, and compels me to show others the whole vivid, complex, unfolding picture of religion in the world that I see. It is so much bigger than the headlines of violence, full of hope in and beyond the despair. And it is so richly equipped to be a vital part of the mix by which we address all of the important issues before us in the twenty-first century. If I do write another book, it will be to continue telling that story.

QUESTIONS FOR DISCUSSION

1. Throughout the book, but most notably in chapter five, Tippett draws a careful distinction between spirituality and religion. Discuss this distinction. How do you define the two?

2. Tippett mentions the theologian Miroslav Volf's ideas of "thick" and "thin" religion. Thin religions tend to reduce their creed to simple cookie-cutter formulas. How would you characterize the religious traditions you grew up in, or those in your community today?

3. A key point repeated in *Speaking of Faith* is that science without religion, and vice versa, can provide only an incomplete picture of the world. Discuss this with reference to Einstein and Darwin, as Tippett does, or with reference to any other scientist you are familiar with.

4. *Ubuntu* is a central virtue in this book. Where besides chapter five is this virtue expressed? How much importance do you give this virtue in your own life?

5. The Tomb of Abraham, which is shared by both Jews and Muslims, is presented as a model for peace conflicts everywhere. Discuss the uneasy peace that is described by Bruce Feiler in the book. Do you think this is the best we can hope for?

6. As Tippett demonstrates, words and phrases like love and moral values are so overused that they no longer carry real meaning for us. She reintroduces the word *edifying* to our moral vocabulary. Are there other words or phrases that should be dropped or restored to our conversations about virtue?

7. *Speaking of Faith* reminds us that whatever language we use to express faith, the divine, or spirituality will ultimately fail. Words can only be approximations for things that are and will always be ineffable to human experience. What do you think is the proper relationship between language and religion?

8. This book reminds us of the central importance the New Testament places on the virtue of hospitality, which is often overlooked today. Are there other virtues—Jewish, Christian, Muslim—that are being ignored today? Which virtues are currently held in disproportionately higher esteem than others?

9. One hard lesson to swallow is that suffering is part of God's kingdom. This notion is shared by the Buddhist monk Thich Nhat Hanh as well as the medieval historian Margaret Spufford. What do you think about their interpretation of the existence of suffering? Does it run counter to the prevailing ideas in your community, or in the country?

10. Tippett makes the point that we often think of religion as constituted by what a person believes, not necessarily what a person practices. She notes that Islam stresses action as much as belief. Do you think Americans emphasize belief at the expense of action or practice? In what way?

11. The author encounters several religious faiths that do not shy away from the "mess and mystery of the physical." While certainly not embraced by mainstream American religions, there are several traditions in this country that incorporate the physical body in their worship. Discuss your own faith's relationship with the body.

For more information about or to order other Penguin Readers Guides, please e-mail the Penguin Marketing Department at reading@us.penguingroup.com or write to us at:

> Penguin Books Marketing Dept.
> Readers Guides
> 375 Hudson Street
> New York, NY 10014-3657

Please allow 4–6 weeks for delivery.
To access Penguin Readers Guides online, visit the Penguin Group (USA) Web site at www.penguin.com.